D1126542

Drieu la Rochelle

Twayne's World Authors Series

Maxwell A. Smith, Editor of French Literature

Professor Emeritus, The University of Chattanooga

Former Visiting Professor in Modern Languages
The Florida State University

TWAS 664

DRIEU LA ROCHELLE
Photograph by Gisèle Freund at Ibiza, Summer 1933.

Drieu la Rochelle

By Robert Barry Leal

The University of Wollongong, Australia

Twayne Publishers • Boston

Drieu la Rochelle

Robert Barry Leal

Published by Twayne Publishers
A Division of G. K. Hall & Company
70 Lincoln Street
Boston, Massachusetts 02111

Book Production by Marne B. Sultz

Book Design by Barbara Anderson

Printed on permanent/durable acid-free
paper and bound in the United States of
America.

**Library of Congress Cataloging in
Publication Data**

Leal, Robert Barry.
Drieu la Rochelle.

(Twayne's world authors series ; TWAS
664)
Bibliography: p. 150
Includes index.
1. Drieu la Rochelle, Pierre, 1893–1945—
Criticism and interpretation.
I. Title. II. Series.
PQ1607.R5Z748 843'.912 82-6055
ISBN 0-8057-6510-7 AACR2

For Roslyn

Contents

About the Author

Robert Barry Leal was educated at the University of Sydney and the University of Queensland and holds the degrees of M.A. and Ph.D. After several years in France in the early 1960s, he returned to Australia and began his tertiary teaching at the University of Queensland. He is currently Professor of French and Chairman of the Department of European Languages at the University of Wollongong in the State of New South Wales. He has published principally in the area of twentieth century French literature (Drieu la Rochelle, Camus, Malraux) but also on the nineteenth century novel (Flaubert). This is Dr. Leal's second book on Drieu la Rochelle, the first, *Drieu la Rochelle: Decadence in Love,* having been published in 1973 by the University of Queensland Press.

Preface

Since the mid-1970s there has been an explosion of interest in the life and work of Pierre Drieu la Rochelle. In 1976 Gallimard began reprinting and reediting all Drieu's unavailable works and by January 1979 this had reached such a stage as to permit Frédéric Grover to say: "The works of few authors of his generation are as readily available as his."[1] In late 1978 a biography of Drieu by an ex-Communist Dominique Desanti, aroused widespread interest, while in 1979 the long-awaited authoritative biography by Frédéric Grover and Pierre Andreu was published. To these two important works should be added the excellent thesis by Julien Hervier on Drieu and Ernst Jünger, published in 1978. Moreover, the relatively recent studies by Robert Soucy and Thomas Hines are indications of the considerable interest in Drieu in the United States, where he has become a not uncommon subject for higher degree theses. On the more popular level, Pierre Granier-Deferre's adaptation of *Une femme à sa fenêtre,* released in 1976, was the second feature-length film to be based on Drieu's works, Louis Malle's *Le Feu follet* having appeared in 1963. All these manifestations of a resurgence of interest in Drieu suggest that his period of literary "purgatory" has ended.

Studies on Drieu have, up to the present, largely focused on him as an historical figure. This is particularly so within France, where the fascination exerted by his view of contemporary society as decadent, his political commitment to fascism, and his role as "collaborator" during the German occupation have tended to impede an appreciation of his literary importance. As Jacqueline Lévi-Valensi once said of much critical reaction to Camus: "It is as if it were more a question of defining oneself in relation to him than striving for a better understanding of his work."[2] With the possible exception of Julien Hervier's comparative study, which gives interesting insights into Drieu's literature of imagination, the only published works exclusively devoted to Drieu as a literary figure have come from outside France.

In focusing almost solely on Drieu's imaginative writing, the present study does not simply seek to redress this imbalance and evaluate

Drieu's excellence as a literary artist. It also aims, by accepting Drieu's fictional world on its own terms and treating it within its own framework, to compose a picture of the author that will serve to complement and at times rectify the picture that has been presented of Drieu the "historical figure." If Proust is correct in his statement that "a book is the product of a self different from the one that we display in society,"[3] then it is reasonable to assume that any study which either neglects the works of a person's imagination or uses them as a mere "quarry" for confirmation or even elucidation will inevitably produce a vision of the person that is either truncated or misleading.

Limitations of space have precluded the possibility of treating all Drieu's fictional work. It has been necessary to exclude the two published plays and also the short stories from different periods contained in *Histoires déplaisantes.* These works supplement the analysis of the works treated but do not add major new elements. On the other hand it has been considered essential for the completeness of the picture presented to include, however briefly, the poetry and poetic portraits of *Interrogation, Fond de cantine,* and *La Suite dans les idées.*

For the purposes of this study the unifying thematic elements in Drieu's imaginative writing have been identified as a conviction of the decadence of contemporary society[4] and an effort to define the relationship of the individual "self" to this society. At times one of these elements appears dominant, at times the other, but on every occasion the portrayal of society and the presentation of the self serve to illuminate each other, even in those works when the author seems farthest from immediate social concerns. Of the strongly autobiographical *Etat civil* Marcel Arland wrote in 1922: "These childhood memories have social ramifications,"[5] and twenty-one years later in *L'Homme à cheval* the degree of involvement of the imaginative writer in social and political action is still an issue of major concern. It is against the fascinating interplay of these notions of self and society that Drieu's development as a literary artist will be traced.

Robert Barry Leal

The University of Wollongong, Australia

Chronology

1893 Pierre-Eugène Drieu la Rochelle born in Paris January 3; both parents of Norman origin.

1903 Birth of brother Jean.

1907 Discovery of Nietzsche.

1908 Holidays in England at Shrewsbury; captivated by English life.

1910 Introspective tendencies encouraged by reading of *Journal* of Amiel. Enrolls concurrently at Ecole des Sciences politiques and Faculty of Law at the Sorbonne. First unsuccessful literary efforts.

1912–1913 Unofficial engagement to Colette Jeramec, sister of his best friend, André.

1913 Fails final political science examinations. Military service: joins the infantry.

1914 August: "mystical" experience at Charleroi during a bayonet charge; Drieu wounded, André Jeramec killed. Composes his first war poems. Death of maternal grandmother Lefèvre.

1915 Active service in the Dardanelles; evacuated with severe dysentery. Reads *Cinq grandes odes* of Claudel.

1916 Father of Colette Jeramec commits suicide. Drieu composes the poems of *Interrogation*. Further hospitalization.

1917 Publication of *Interrogation* despite opposition of censors. Marries Colette Jeramec, who shares her fortune with him.

1918 June: attached to American unit as interpreter.

1919 March: demobilized.

1920 *Fond de cantine.* Divorces Colette Jeramec but remains on good terms throughout his life. Begins to spend freely and travel widely. Friendship with Louis Aragon.

1921 *Etat civil.*

1922 *Mesure de la France.* Meets E. B. ("L'Algérienne"), who becomes his mistress but dies of cancer in late 1923.

1924 *Plainte contre inconnu.*

1925 *L'Homme couvert de femmes.* His mistress, Connie Walsh, returns to America. Death of mother. Break with Aragon.

1927 *La Suite dans les idées. Le jeune Européen.* Marriage to Alexandra Sienkiewicz, daughter of Parisian banker. Seven issues of *Les derniers jours* produced with Emmanuel Berl.

1928 *Blèche. Genève ou Moscou.* Travels to Greece. Friendship with Gaston Bergery.

1929 *Une femme à sa fenêtre.* Meets Victoria Ocampo, Argentinian woman of letters; contributes to *Sur* when founded by Victoria Ocampo in 1931. Visits England. Suicide of his friend Jacques Rigaut. Separates from his wife (divorce in 1933).

1931 *L'Europe contre les patries. Le Feu follet. L'Eau fraîche* (play) presented fifty-two times by Louis Jouvet. Refuses Legion of Honor.

1932 Lecture tour of the Argentine and travel in South America. Develops friendship with Jorge Luis Borges, who provides him with the idea for *L'Homme à cheval.* Growing interest in politics. Lecture tour in Germany.

1933 *Drôle de voyage.*

1934 *La Comédie de Charleroi* (prix de la Renaissance). *Journal d'un homme trompé. Socialisme fasciste.* January: goes with Bertrand de Jouvenel to Berlin, where he meets Otto Abetz, future ambassador to France. February: riots associated with Stavisky scandal encourage Drieu in the belief that the Right and the Left may form a viable political grouping. Collaborates with Bertrand de Jouvenel at *Lutte des jeunes* and declares himself a Fascist. Father dies. Fact-finding visit to Czechoslovakia, Hungary, and Italy. *Le Chef* (play) presented by Pitoëff: only five performances but highly regarded by critics.

1935 Meets "Beloukia" (Christiane Renault) and begins a liaison of ten years. Attends Congress of Nuremberg and then visits Moscow.

1936 *Beloukia. Doriot, ou la vie d'un ouvrier français.* Joins the Fascist-oriented Parti populaire français recently founded by ex-Communist Jacques Doriot; for thirty months writes regularly in *Emancipation nationale,* organ of the party. Visits Berlin, Italy, North Africa, and Franco's Spain. "Nous sommes plusieurs" (unpublished play).

1937 *Rêveuse bourgeoisie. Avec Doriot.*

1937–1938 Starts writing *Gilles.* Begins to speak of his "great political disappointment."

1939 Resigns from Parti populaire français. Visits prehistoric caves at Les Eyzies with abbé Breuil. Increasing interest in the history of religions. After being called up he is discharged medically unfit. Growing anti-Semitism. Quarrel with Jean Paulhan, director of the *Nouvelle revue française,* over the participation of Louis Aragon. December: *Gilles* (censored); integral edition with preface 1942.

1940 *Charlotte Corday* (play) refused by the Théâtre français. Following rumor of imminent arrest, leaves Paris for the Dordogne (La Roque-Gageac). At Vichy offers his services to the government. Interview in Paris with Abetz, who warns him of the harshness of the proposed peace treaty between France and Germany. Prepares to revive the *Nouvelle revue française* in December, Abetz having promised his support. Presents to Abetz the "bande de la banque Worms" as a possible governing group.

1941 *Ecrits de jeunesse. Notes pour comprendre le siècle.* Visits Weimar and Berlin. His fears grow that Hitler is becoming more and more nationalistic and less and less socialistic.

1942 Second presentation at Vichy, Lyon, and Clermont of *Charlotte Corday.* Rejoins Parti populaire français.

1943 *L'Homme à cheval. Chronique politique 1934–1942.* Composes *L'Intermède romain* (long short story). Has his first wife and her two children released after their arrest by the Gestapo. June: publication of the last issue of the *Nouvelle revue française* under Drieu's direction. Increased religious reading and meditation. Mussolini's resignation in July turns Drieu further toward communism; certain of his articles, too favorable to Stalinist Russia, are censored by the Germans. Goes to Switzerland. May 1943–August 1944: regular contributor to *Révolution nationale* of Lucien Combelle.

1944 *Charlotte Corday; Le Chef.* July–August: *Les Chiens de paille* and *Le Français d'Europe* are published but are seized and destroyed. August 1: attempted suicide; a few days later opens his veins but is saved again. September: declines to go to Switzerland; hides with friends in Paris and then goes to the country. Composes *Récit secret* and *Mémoires de Dirk Raspe.*

1945 15–16 March: successful suicide; buried at Neuilly.

1951 *Plaintes contre inconnue* (poems). *Récit secret.*

1963 *Histoires déplaisantes.*

1964 *Sur les écrivains. Les Chiens de paille.*

1966 *Mémoires de Dirk Raspe.*

1979 *Les derniers jours.*

Chapter One
Youthful Writings

Pierre Drieu la Rochelle first came to the notice of the French literary world as a poet of war. Lyrical in form and intensely personal in tone, the poems of *Interrogation,* written between 1915 and 1917, tell of a young man's initial reactions to the experience of war. In 1920 there appeared *Fond de Cantine* [From the Bottom of the Trunk], in which a number of war poems are followed by others expressing a demobilized soldier's attitudes to postwar society. Certain of Drieu's other early writings, also largely poetic in form and most dating from the years following 1918, were published in 1927 under the title *La Suite dans les idées* [Ideas and their Coherence]. In theme and tone these three works form a coherent group and are, in Drieu's words, a poetic reaction "to the war and to the initial aspects of peace viewed by a man returning from the war and still imbued with it."[1] War is not so overtly present in *Le jeune Européen* [The Young European], also published in 1927 and grouped with the previous three works in 1941 under the title *Ecrits de jeunesse* [Youthful Writings], but the attitudes of the narrator and the issues that are discussed are explicable only against the background of the conflict of the preceding years.

It was thus the experience of war that launched Drieu into literature, first as poet, then as prose writer. It was an experience which frequently evoked in him mixed feelings of nostalgia and which constitutes the principal point of reference, at times clearly visible and at others merely implied, of his works about the society of the interwar period. As he wrote in the 1940s: "And after all, perhaps that is all I have ever had to talk about and everything else has been simply indirect allusion or superfluous padding."[2]

Interrogation

The four sections of *Interrogation* all treat overtly the experience of war, and very self-consciously exalt the virile virtues that open conflict among men demands. There is, however, a development clearly perceptible from one section to another, and, as the title implies, a questioning of what ramifications the intensity discovered in war will have on French society when the war is finished. The title refers to the questioning by the poet of himself, as he seeks to understand the significance of his enthusiasm for war. Hence, already in *Interrogation* there is an indication of those tensions involving the self and society which characterize all Drieu's literature. Of *Interrogation* he later said: "I am one of those who project themselves completely into their first book. The cry that I uttered in it is the essence of what I have to say."[3]

The very first poem, "Paroles au départ" [Parting Words], proclaims action as necessary for spiritual and intellectual health. Strength is termed by the poet "the life-blood of my thought" and the front is regarded as a religious retreat to which men have repaired to meditate on the significance of life. Here, as in some of the other poems, action takes on an integrative function, perhaps best expressed in the implicit hope of the opening line: "Both dream and action." Action brings an experience of the fullness of life, and with it a sense of value: "I know what I am worth and what value is."

It is, however, not just physical activity that the poet relishes in war but unalloyed violence.[4] Initially the violence of war is directed against the poet's own body:

> Strength is before me, a foundation stone. I must
> feel its resistance, it must strike my bones.
> I must be crushed.

Associated with this masochistic need of suffering is the attraction of death, which, through the voluptuous fear it produces, is seen as opening to man "the secret of life." In "Tryptique de la mort" [Triptych of Death], composed in the hospital after the death of two comrades, the poet's obsession with death and suffering becomes quite pathological. He sees himself living constantly in the expectation of its coming, devoting every thought to it and finally experiencing at the moment of death a sense of eternity as he is struck down in a "paroxysm of beauty" on the barbed wire of the enemy lines.

In certain of the poems of *Interrogation* Drieu expresses the hope that the uncompromising violence of war will also permeate social life in peacetime. "We shall be demanding," he warns in "Caserne haïe"

[Detested Barracks], and calls for the destruction of the old order and the installation of one that is new and creative. This rather naive enthusiasm for the new, apparent also in certain poems of Drieu's wartime contemporary Apollinaire, illustrates the influence of the "Futurist" movement centered on Marinetti. Such influence—or at least the influence of the vocabulary attaching to it—was acknowledged by Drieu and led to his adoption of the term "eternal futurism"[5] to describe his attitude. He claimed to welcome the modern and the new not necessarily in their present expressions but rather as manifestations of life's creative processes at work. This distinction, difficult as it was to sustain in practice (since it gave little scope to aesthetic or moral discrimination), is of key importance in understanding the tensions of Drieu's thought. It kept alive in him an openness and enthusiasm toward new movements and ideas that he was nevertheless constantly obliged to temper on moral and aesthetic grounds. He expressed the problem succinctly in "A vous Allemands" [To You Germans] by describing human life and history as "that delicate balance between barbarity and civilization."

The awareness that in postwar France the decadence of prewar days may in fact continue and intensify comes to disconcert the warrior's enthusiasm and ultimately leads him to castigate rather than welcome the products of the modern age. Drieu's obsession with modern decadence is born. It is an attitude that he will hold with increasing conviction throughout the interwar period. For him creativity works through the explosive and destructive force of the "idea," which leads mankind's elite to great enterprises, dragging the largely passive "female crowd" ("Restauration du corps" [Restoration of the Body]) in its train. While never quite abandoning his search for such creative ideas and such an elite, Drieu came to believe that the modern age had failed to produce either.

In the fourth section of *Interrogation,* and also in part of the third, the intellectual side of the poet's personality asserts itself as he seeks to understand and evaluate the concepts, ideas, and obsessions that have emerged in his poetry. His aim is at once sociological, psychological, and philosophical. He wishes to determine the extent to which he as an individual has absorbed and is now expressing the social currents of his time, while at the same time he is intent on exploring the relationship between personal preoccupations and the concept he holds of man's eternal nature.

Such sociological and broad psychological rationalizations, however, do not account for the obsession with death as an absolute that we have noted above, and they fail to explain the intensity of the poet's masochism in battle.[6] These are traits that relate to the psychology of the particular individual. At this point Drieu makes no effort to analyze these aberrations of personality, but in "Interrogation de la paix" [A Questioning of Peace] he does attempt to analyze one of the psychological conflicts of which he is keenly aware: the disharmony between the convictions of his intelligence and the reactions of his body. His distress comes from the fact that, despite the exultation he feels under fire at the front, his body cannot suppress a cry of revolt against the suffering or death that threaten. This age-old complaint, in the tradition of Pascal, St. Augustine, and St. Paul, at the conflict between spirit and flesh leads to the question of the integration of his personality, to problems of personal identity, and to the suggestion that he contains not one but several truths:

> There was that cry from my flesh, that groan from
> my stomach and there were also the venerable words
> of my intelligence.
> And before it, who am I?

This cry of distress tends to be submerged by the other preoccupations of *Interrogation,* but it remains as one of the issues to emerge from the experience of war and is taken up in the pages of *Etat civil* [Civil Status].

Fond de cantine

Several poems of *Fond de cantine* [Bottom of the Locker] were composed at the same time as those of *Interrogation,* but the collection generally speaking shows a perceptible development of ideas and a clearer focusing of certain of the themes expressed in the earlier poems. As the poet's direct experience of war fades into the realm of nostalgic memory, the problems faced by the individual and his society in postwar Europe become more and more pressing. In particular Drieu's conviction of personal and social decadence grows in intensity.

Woman plays an increasingly important role in the first section of *Fond de cantine,* where she appears more and more as a direct threat to the desire to maintain the memory and the values of war. Whereas in *Interrogation* woman had been pictured at times in an idealized role and at others as something to be totally rejected, now her continuing presence and attraction are simply resented. She becomes a much more subtle creature: Eve-like, she is a persistent temptation to the male to turn from his ideas of duty.

The misogyny of *Fond de cantine* illustrates the poet's consciousness that the values of war extolled in *Interrogation* are slipping from his grasp. Fraternity among men and loyalty to one's country are proclaimed as superior to love between man and woman, but such statements appear as desperate attempts to preserve ideals rather than as confidently held attitudes. In these poems we are in fact witnessing some of the first expressions of one of the principal themes of Drieu's postwar fictional literature. It is the "permanent ambiguity" which Bernard Vorge describes in these terms: "All his male characters, [. . .] both seek out and scorn women, and persecute them for not reflecting back to them the desired image."[7] Such impossible demands are, however, to some degree counterbalanced by the more violent emotion of scorn directed by the poet at himself and his society for their failures. Invariably in Drieu's writing scorn is accompanied by a desire to destroy, and this psychological reflex emerges clearly in three of the poems of this collection. In "Péroraison" [Peroration], which has many affinities with his "Exorde" [Exordium] of 1943, Drieu masochistically pictures himself expiating his lack of heroism by a horrible death, thus achieving a final beauty denied him in life; in the bitterly ironic "Vengeance" he calls down upon himself and his pathetic companions in decadence the wrath of the god of war and revolution; and in "Révolution" he calls upon a strong, merciless leader to restore virility and health to the "soulless body" of the aimless feminine crowd.

The call for strong leadership in "Révolution" draws attention to Drieu's growing conviction that the tendency to decadence can be redressed only through violence, since the masses are of themselves incapable of taking such initiative. Drieu's profoundly undemocratic outlook generally extends, in fact, to seeking salvation completely outside the society. The need for a certain "barbarity" to keep civilization healthy was noted in passing in *Interrogation,* but now it assumes greater urgency, and non-European intervention comes to be considered essential.

In the two poems of the final section of *Fond de cantine* Drieu turns prophet and presents certain aspects of Western life as he sees it developing in the twentieth century. The verses of "Auto" depict the car as "Action reduced to its essence." It is the means by which modern man is enabled to experience the exhilaration of speed and to relish a sense of power. Roads penetrate to all corners of the earth, which is now spread forth before him like a map waiting to be explored. But the enthusiasm for power, speed, and discovery is considerably tempered by other preoccupations in the poem, and the final impression conveyed is that the car is not so much an agent of liberation as one of destruction and evasion. It parts the embrace of earth and sky in its flight forward and destroys the tranquillity of nature:

> I shatter horizons.
> The partitions of the sky are burst.
> The soul of the landscape dispersed.

The poems of *Fond de cantine* are in general less starkly personal than those of *Interrogation* and considerably less lyrical in tone. They present reflections rather than enthusiasms and for the most part express fear, resentment, and irony about a distasteful present rather than a firm determination to mold the future. This change of tone doubtless accounts for the experimentation in form of the collection. Numerous examples of free verse with strong rhythm are still to be found, but so also are poems of a more traditional structure with regular meter and a strict rhyming scheme. This is an evident attempt by Drieu to discover the form appropriate to his subject and to convey the more somber note of his preoccupations now that the lyrical aspects of life are to be found almost solely in the memory. The resultant poetry holds considerable interest, but much more because of the ideas expressed and the very fact of the experimentation than because of the form chosen. Indeed, quite often the form of the poetry, especially the use of rhyme, detracts from the expression of ideas, making them appear somewhat shallow and trite. Drieu's poetic talents lie in the realm of the lyrical and his poetry tends to decline in quality as he moves from this realm and from the forms most appropriate to its expression.

La Suite dans les idées

La Suite dans les idées [Coherence in One's Ideas] is an oddly assorted collection of poems, confessions, parables, and short stories of the postwar years. As the title suggests, it is a continuation, and to some degree a development, of ideas expressed in Drieu's earlier work. The now-familiar themes are all present: nostalgia for war; the emasculating effects of women and peacetime pleasures; distress at the body's inability to rise to the height of the "idea"; and the need for strong leadership. The chief importance of the work, however, lies in the area of literary form and structure. The years from 1918 to 1927 were for Drieu a period of literary quest, experimentation and discovery, and these processes appear more clearly in *La Suite dans les idées* than in other works. Here we have a privileged glimpse of the writer at work, developing the tools and techniques that he will use in the major novels and short stories of the late 1920s and the 1930s. In his "Preamble" he confesses to his reader that he has not the strength to forge the pell-mell of his "vague ideas" into a "fine metal tool, elegant and strong, to pierce your heart, to sparkle in the sun." The various elements of *La Suite dans les idées* nevertheless show that he was moving to this goal.

The "Preamble" is a rather melodramatic confession by the writer of impotence and inadequacy in the important areas of life and a rather contrived admission that he has chosen to retreat to the trivial: "Neither warrior, nor athlete, nor husband, nor poet, nor priest, I have made myself a scribe." But even at this level the writer views himself as a caricature of what he would like to be. He not only finds the heights of poetry denied him, but is also incapable of creating noble characters for works of prose. The final two paragraphs give the confession an ironic twist and demonstrate a technique that will be fully exploited in the future. The writer, having bewailed his own incapacity in sackcloth and ashes, invites the reader to recognize himself or his contemporaries in the portrait painted. This technique, used with consummate skill many years later by Camus in *La Chute* [The Fall], is employed rather clumsily on this occasion by Drieu. It does, however, constitute a significant step toward the successful marriage of confession and social criticism that marks the Gille novels.

This nostalgic farewell to war is followed by five "parables of the return," in which the straightforward statement, confession, and lament of previous works give way to a fictional approach, realistic description mingling with surrealistic image.[8] The least enigmatic of the five parables, "Le Sergent de ville" [The Town Policeman], is dedicated to André Breton, and the people it depicts may well be several of the leading Surrealists of the 1920s. The influence of the latter on Drieu's writing is quite apparent in "Le Dictateur" [The Dictator]. Here he treats the theme of the passive, vulgar crowd's need of a strong, virile leader. A young athletic trapeze artist–cum–pilot lands a plane on the roof of a music hall, crashes his way through the glass dome, thrills the cowering crowd with his acrobatic skill, and, after threatening them with machine guns, disappears into the heavens with his troop of young men and his booty of beautiful girls. This fanciful episode is one of the few examples of the use by Drieu of Surrealist techniques. It is an interesting experiment, but one that was obviously rejected, since it appears only rarely in his later writing. The theme of the strong leader is also treated in "La Gymnastique suédoise" [Swedish Gymnastics] (retitled "Autre dictateur" [A Different Dictator] in *Ecrits de jeunesse*) in roughly the form of a short philosophical tale, and again in "Demi-tour à droite" [Right Turn], where the free play of the imagination in the previous two tales yields to the realism of life in army barracks. These three parables of the necessity of strong leadership are not intrinsically of great literary merit. They do, however, provide a highly illuminating example of Drieu's search for an adequate vehicle for his ideas in the early postwar years: they treat the same theme in three quite different literary forms.

"Une île au nom de femme" [An Island Called Woman], "Oasis," and "Grandeur et persécution" [Greatness and Persecution] treat the poet's relationship to woman. Here, as in so many other aspects of his life, he is tormented by his inability to find a correspondence in reality to the ideal image that his mind conceives. His "île au nom de femme" is found far from the "port of lucre" that is Paris, across the seas of solitude. No sooner is it reached, however, than its substantiality collapses before him.

> With your subterranean cry, woman, o hole of misery,
> Dull fire from which there issues a deceptive odor
> You have guided me, you have drawn me to your hell.

At other times the poet regards himself as a "great spoiler of booty," incapable of drawing from woman the treasures she holds. This classic Western conflict in its view of woman: *femme fatale* or source of man's inspiration, seductive Eve or holy Virgin-Mother, is felt very keenly by Drieu and consciously or unconsciously informs much of his literary production. Since fear of woman as seductress makes impossible any firm and enduring commitment, the poet, despite his tendency to idealize woman, is condemned to be a Don Juan of perpetual flight. It is for this reason that solitude is associated in this section with the ideal image of woman: she can have reality only insofar as she is dissociated from the real world of social intercourse. Ultimately she becomes merely a product of the writer's imagination.

Drieu is at his most bitter in "Mesure de la France" [France's Capabilities], a page-long description of "the most civilized man in the world": a Frenchman as he emerges from a village urinal. His church closed, his history forgotten, and his village depopulated, the man represents the lack of creativity that Drieu sees as characterizing his time. "Une ville d'Europe" [A European Town] and "Coucher sous les ponts" [Sleeping under the Bridges] focus more specifically on decadence in man's aesthetic appreciation and creative abilities. Here there is little of the enthusiasm for the modern which had led Drieu to accept the term "eternal futurism." Though such a doctrine is not denied (since to reject it would engender complete despair), Drieu is forced to recognize that in modern times there is little evidence of the creative spirit. The sources of man's creativity are dry, the Holy Spirit having "withdrawn beneath the earth, into the sap of the plants which alone still continue to burst forth each spring."

"Découvertes" [Discoveries], the final section of *La Suite dans les idées* (but not included in *Ecrits de jeunesse*), contains two of Drieu's fairly early attempts at the short story. The first, entitled "L'Aumône" [The Act of Charity], is clearly superior to "Le seul bonheur" [The Only Happiness], ideas being better integrated into the story and situations appearing not nearly so contrived. Both stories treat the subject of contemporary man-woman relationships, examining the reactions of two men to an idealized female figure. In "L'Aumône" the superficiality of the postwar years served as a background to the unlikely relationship that develops between the worldly young Hugues and the physically unattractive Mlle de Ménerles. This woman, of unspecified age, achieves her stature as an ideal figure precisely by her silent judgment of the unseemly conduct of those who come to visit her. For Hugues, still suffering from a sentimental misadventure for which he blames himself, she represents a combination of femininity and moral strength. She displays "a warrior's mercy which grasps one by both shoulders." At the end of the story she is left in her lonely isolation, though now with the hope of a child, as Hugues flees from a situation that might bring responsibility and restriction. This episode successfully combines many of the themes treated in the early section of *La Suite dans les idées*. Now, however, they are incorporated in a way that does not disturb the simple unity of the short story and indicates that the writer is close to achieving mastery of this literary form.

Le jeune Européen

In an age in which form and structure in all areas of life are seen as becoming progressively less distinct, the young man who gives *Le jeune Européen*[9] its title seeks to understand the conflicting tendencies of his personality by probing his "self" and by determining its relation to the outside world. More specifically, he tries to come to terms with the misgivings he has about his inclination to write. The title of the first of the two sections, "Le Sang et l'encre" [Blood and Ink], indicates clearly enough the basic dilemma. How does one who considers man to be essentially a creature of action reconcile such a view with a desire for the solitude of literary creation? Is literature, above all that which cannot escape preoccupation with the self, necessarily a retreat from life, a denial of man's completeness? Such questions, foreshadowing in large measure those posed by adepts of "literature of commitment" later in the century and by Drieu's own novels of the 1940s, are followed in the second section of the book by a series of images of contemporary society which center upon the music hall and explore the concept of decadence.

Although the later sections of "Le Sang et l'encre" contain specific reference to Drieu's own literary works, there is a determined initial attempt to generalize the experience of the narrator by making him a European rather than a French figure and by causing him to run the gamut of European civilization and its various offshoots throughout the world. The young European is born in France, but his paternity is unknown. Was his father English, or Russian, or French? All that is certain is that his father was white and probably European, since his mother, spurning national boundaries, moves within the broader confines of Europe, bestowing her favors on men of all nationalities and accepting their largesse. Heir to this supranational disposition, the young European pursues his education at Paris, Cambridge, and Jena and complements his reading of Bergson, Claudel, Gide, and Barres with d'Annunzio, Kipling, and Nietzsche. The war brings, indirectly, the opportunity for flight to the United States, thence to Russia, and passing reference is also made to India and China. Everywhere the determining influence of Europe is to be found. Americans are merely "the worst Europeans who have changed continents to enjoy at greater leisure their game of brutes taken over by the abstract" (186);[10] Russia, with its state-based capitalism, remains subject to "the fearful Western discipline" (188); and China and India vary little from this distressing pattern. Having encircled the globe, witnessed and savored the various manifestations of European civilization as prewar playboy, disillusioned soldier, successful businessman, and Bolshevik revolutionary, the young European returns to peacetime Paris to reflect upon his experiences and to adapt to a less frenetic life-style.

The world-encircling adventures of the young European, situated in the period 1912–1922, provide Drieu with the opportunity not only of expressing in fictional form his views on the ramifications of contemporary European civilization but also of depicting the nature of this civilization through his literary style. The short, sharp sentences and paragraphs, together with the wealth of confused, unelaborated sense impressions conveyed by images that often startle with their evocative power, illustrate the frantic superficial search for sensation that, for the narrator, characterized the decade depicted. "My insatiable appetite demanded every dream and every action" (180), cries the young European. He seeks to satisfy this hunger first "by furiously rushing across a Europe that was for [him] simply a big toy that [he] would have liked to break" (180); then in the "patrols, mine warfare, brutish wild comradeship, sordid glory" (181) of his "Orphic travels in a realm so strongly male" (184); in the "mocking labyrinth of corridors" (185) of his New York prison; and finally among the "people of peasant dancers" (186) in Russia. Statements designed to shock by their brutality alternate with mystical aspirations, while from time to time a yearning after the harsh and the physical yields to the soft attractions of more civilized living. Moreover, the image of an age in which "men still believed in the individual" (180) is evoked stylistically by the repetition of the first-person pronoun, especially at the beginning of sentences. Such is the world view and the nature of the young European on whom we are invited to reflect in the later chapters of the work, as immobility succeeds movement, and the world of literature replaces the stimulation of physical action.

The sense of loneliness and isolation produced by relative inactivity in Paris leads to an unavoidable confrontation with the self and its relation to a dying society. Do the individual's shortcomings, his inability to adapt to his age or to continue to pursue the vitality glimpsed during his decade of adventures, result from inherent tendencies or are they rather the reflection of a decadent society? This question is pursued specifically within the framework of literature. What influence does the world of books have on the avidly reading child? Does it encourage him to live in a realm of images and ideas and impede the developing consciousness of the world of concrete objects? Does literature, read or written, sap the vitality of the individual and encourage the lethargy that afflicts the young European of the 1920s? Does literature truncate man's natural development and confine him to the world of the self? Is there, in short, antinomy between writing and living?

No final satisfactory answers are given to these questions, but their investigation enables the narrator to deepen the concept he has of the self and in so doing to find a tentative justification for his writing. Probing of the self is no longer seen as mere narcissism. The "subterranean realms" (201) of the self provide access to the more fundamental elements of life and society, and these the writer may explore. "My self," claims the young European, "is no longer the individual in society, but the universe marked with the seal of man, one last time" (214). In particular the suggestion is made that a sense of the reality of others may be attained through a probing of the self. The young European's friends are recognized by him as "secret parts of my consciousness" (210), their reality more accessible to the probings of reflective art than to the photographic pretensions of Realism.

These reflections, with their conclusions rather tentatively expressed (mainly because of the irrepressible urge to violent action that frequently comes surging back), are of considerable significance on several levels. On the most obvious level, we are presented with the intellectual odyssey of a particular writer striving to reconcile his creative literary talents with a firmly held ideal of the nature of man. The reader is provided, moreover, with a privileged glimpse of the writer at work, sharing in the enthusiasms, hesitations, frustrations, and disappointments of creation.

The representative nature of the young European, however, which Drieu was at pains to establish in the opening chapter of the book, transposes this individual experience to a far more general level. In an age characterized by frenetic but aimless activity, "Le Sang et l'encre" presents the efforts of a young European intellectual both to find his way through the multitude of movements and influences that marked the postwar period and to establish the position of the literary artist. The call to violent heroic action mediated through the works of Nietzsche produces a questioning of the very activity of writing and arouses the suspicion that the study-bound intellectual is but half a man. The rejection of the restrictive individualism of the early Barrès and of a Gide is seen in the young European's initial efforts to reach beyond the confines of the self, while the later discovery that the self is far profounder than suspected reveals the influence of the general current of ideas interpreted, among others, by Bergson and Proust and by certain of the Surrealists.

As a background to these tensions there remains the need to situate oneself, however tenuously, within a certain literary tradition, and it is for this reason that a lineage is sought through Barrès, Chateaubriand, and Rousseau, and finally back to Montaigne. In this way "Le Sang et l'encre" has, like *Etat civil,* both an individual and a representative value, providing a further example of Drieu's attempts to combine, through the autobiographical form, generalized social comment with personal discovery and confession.

By the end of "Le Sang et l'encre" the young European appears to have reached an acceptance of his activity as writer, but at the same time he stresses that this does not deprive him of the possibility of acting in other ways: he remains "a man who is a prey to the total problem" (213). His freedom consists of adopting toward his writing and life itself an attitude of close involvement that stops short of being total. He needs to retain the possibility of "a mystical opening" and hence determines to "give the closest attention to all this detail that is the world, and also to be ready to let everything drop."[11] Such is the working compromise to which his reflections lead him.

In his initial description of the music hall in the second section of *Le jeune Européen,* Drieu avoids the tendency to abstraction that constantly threatens a satirist by contrasting this house of shallow amusement with an image of the Church in previous ages. In a passage announcing the idealization of the Middle Ages that will increasingly appear in his later works, he depicts the Church as having given a spiritual centrality to man's life and drawn him into close communion with his fellows. Its unchanging rites and its use of the Latin common to all Christendom enabled the individual of medieval times, and especially the lonely foreigner, to transcend local and national boundaries. In the twentieth century the music hall likewise extends across Europe and its satellites, but it by contrast degrades the individual. Spiritual aspiration gives way to tawdry diversion, and the close sense of community which encouraged individual self-respect is replaced by "an immense ill-defined communism, comfortable, boring, ugly" (234). The ramifications of this imaginative contrast are seen throughout the description of this modern "faceless temple" (218), as the young European passes from contemplation of the ugliness of its uninspired architecture to observe its tasteless interior and comment scathingly on those whom it attracts. At its entrance "seedy-looking angels [. . .] see to the placing of the humans in these heavens" (219) before the "rite" begins. "The faithful are about to fill the temple" (222), each "Adam" with his "Eve" forming a "genesis no man has ever imagined" (222). But this is "a temple no longer frequented by gods or priests" (230): it is a spiritual vacuum in which men seek distraction from the emptiness of their lives.

The bitter satire conveyed by such images as these at times brings the young European to the brink of thoroughgoing misanthropy and even destructive nihilism. However, through his apocalyptic imaginings a frustrated idealism is clearly visible. The young European's frustration comes from a fundamental belief in man's spiritual and creative capacities, which in the modern age are denied expression.

The central dialogue of "Le Music-hall" between "me" and "the other" is in reality a monologue by the young European between two aspects of his personality. In it he seeks to confront and to come to terms in a rational manner with the more extreme aspects of his approach to modern life. The distressed pessimism of "me," whose belief in modern decadence is expressed in the formula "today is bad, tomorrow will be worse, [. . .] it will all be over tomorrow" (236), is countered in dialectic fashion by the faith of "the other" in an unpredictable future. "The other" faces with equanimity the prospect of a dehumanized world, which he depicts in terms that recall Huxley's *Brave New World.* Moreover, he claims to see already "emerging through the thickness of living ugliness, new confusing beauties" (247). The desperate attachment of "moi" to what he sees as essentially human, and as such irreplaceable, is presented with considerable force. He is not prepared to offer upon the altar of some indeterminate future the values inherent in the high points of art, love, religion, and war.

Such efforts to adopt a more rational approach to what is fundamentally a passionate conviction of decadence lead him to an attitude of uneasy acceptance, indeed to a tenuous tranquillity translated in the very last paragraph into delicate images of nature and religion:

But the forest adorns the hermit's retreat and puts flowers in his beard. Has the time of the poverty of the saints come? Job, sitting amid ruins with your possessions shattered, perhaps God will rebuild your house. Pleasant smell of the planet as of an apple in my hand. (272)

Le jeune Européen, with its two complementary and similarly structured sections, marks a highly important stage in Drieu's literary development. In the first place it shows an effort to understand his role as a writer in postwar Europe, a farewell—though a very reluctant one—to the youthful enthusiasms and extravagances associated with war. The imaginative writer is recognized as having his own valid social role alongside those who pursue a more active physical career. Second, there is a recognition of the futility of refusing the reality of one's age, of judging the relative from the harsh standpoint of the absolute and, like Jonah, calling down the wrath of Heaven upon a decadent Nineveh. The writer has a social function, even though it be that of a blind prophet proclaiming an uncertain message. In the words of the young European: "But I suppose my lot is to work in my age and fail to know it, to reject the present so that, by the office I blindly fulfill, the future may be given form [. . .]" (260). Third, there is the claim that by probing the depths of his self the writer is able to present an authentic image of the realities of life. The young European sees himself as enshrining some of the deepest tendencies of the age and it is the prophetic role of proclaiming these that he henceforth assigns himself.

Résumé

The transition from *Interrogation* to *Fond de cantine* and then to *La Suite dans les idées* and *Le jeune Européen* illustrates, in the area of both subject and form, the collapse of youthful enthusiasms and aspirations and a growing consciousness in the young writer that he must come to terms with the age in which he lives, adopting and developing the means of expression appropriate to it. At the same time, however, the experiences of war and demobilization force him to confront the enigmas of his self and to explore its claims on the society whose values it instinctively rejects. Drieu pursues these twin concerns in the works that follow, as he moves into the field of the novel and develops the art of the short story.

Chapter Two
The Search for Literary Structures

Etat civil

Etat civil, Drieu's first extended prose work, was published in 1921. It is written in the first person and recounts various aspects of the narrator's life from initial self-awareness to the age of sixteen, when his character and attitudes are considered to have been immutably fixed. The work is presented in three parts: the first to the age of eight, in which the immediate family of the child, who is given the name of little Cogle, plays a dominant role; the second showing the child's reaction to the schooling he received; and the third covering the period of early adolescence and also containing many reflections of a generalized nature that refer to later events in his life.

Quite early in the work it is recognized that there are insuperable difficulties in faithfully presenting a mentality and a personality that belong to the past. Barely has the narrator begun to relate his earliest recollections than disconcerting questions intrude to destroy the illusion of authenticity: "Did I see this garden with the same eyes that now see this table? Was I someone else whose strangeness to me now is like the effects of sleep?" (11). At the end of the first part he looks back with vague astonishment at the "mysterious little corpse" (88) that he has exhumed, wondering at its identity. Moreover, at the beginning of the third part, where reminiscence tends to give way to critical comment on the present, he recognizes that "on each page of this book my present life, which is so dear to me and which presses so hard against the walls of my being, flows back on to the splendors of my past" (155). Here we have a recognition of the fundamental dilemma of the autobiographer: the inevitable distortion of the past by the present.

Such recognition of the fictional aspects of any presentation of one's own past informs the whole fabric of *Etat civil,* which gradually reveals itself to be more complex, both in subject and structure, than it at first appears. Doubt about the authenticity of recollection of the past is accompanied by increasing speculation on the importance of such things as race, heredity, and environment, so that the book emerges as an investigation, in autobiographical form, of a number of personal, social, and political ideas. Consequently, though this "strangely premature autobiographical essay," as Drieu later described it,[1] may contain valuable insights for the biographer of Drieu's childhood and youth, it remains self-consciously a basically fictional work of ideas, which exploits the autobiographical form. The narrator does in fact refer to the work at one stage specifically as a novel.

The narrator's intentions in presenting aspects of his past are, moreover, clearly stated as going beyond mere nostalgic recollection: his past life is presented with a specific personal and social aim in mind. Toward the end of the work when his vision of his self has been presented, he states his aim as being "to fix outside myself everything from which I wish to separate myself" (178), and in a similar but more specific vein, he writes of his goal as being "to rid me of myself, or of a self that I was especially during a certain war" (177). The view of the past is designed to serve the future. He writes to "commit [his] future" (141) and dedicates the work to men "between twenty and forty" (166), inviting them to recognize themselves and perform a similar process of exorcism. In the final analysis *Etat civil* may be seen as an interesting literary attempt to combine personal confession with social statement.

At the very outset of little Cogle's recollection the problem of the unity of the self is posed. Not only is there an unbridgeable gap between past consciousness and present recollection, but present recollection itself lays bare an image of the self that is hopelessly divided. Reflecting on his life up to the age of six, Cogle speaks of "those little characters who bore my name" (14), and this multiplicity of the self is a preoccupation that continues throughout the work. The theme of the lack of unity of the self was, of course, extremely fertile for the literary world of the first half of the twentieth century and certain of the literary devices exploited by it are used by Drieu, notably that of the mirror. The mirror is associated with the coming of self-consciousness, the separation of one aspect of the self from its surroundings, and the beginnings of tension and duplicity. It announces, for example, the birth of the "idea" with its capacity to inspire men to those deeds against which the body rebels. Before the mirror young Cogle becomes "double" (12) and, like certain of Drieu's later characters, spends "long moments" (33) before it, reflecting on the person that he is.

The mirror is, of course, merely a literary device to convey a psychological experience, and it is recognized as such as young Cogle seeks to find reasons for the intensity of his inner conflicts. First, tensions within the circle of the family are sought, as he speculates on such things as the mixture of Catholic and liberal elements in his grandmother's background and upbringing; the contrast between her tales of grandeur and heroism and the protected life he is forced to live; and his general distress at the progressive decline in initiative and bravery from one generation to the next. Then questions of social class are raised: he reflects upon the conflicting influences exercised by his bourgeois family and the various peasant women who raised him. Finally, intellectual and social factors are suggested and "a particular French way of thinking" (138) in which he was educated is contrasted with the salutary influences of Nietzsche, Whitman, Kipling, Jack London, and d'Annunzio.

The narrator is, however, somewhat reluctant to consider these aspects of his early life as clearly determining influences on his conduct and personality, since he wishes to preserve the possibility of individual initiative and decision. In his approach to this age-old problem of free will, he adopts a posture of what can best be termed "hesitant determinism." At times, aspects of his early environment are seen as determinants, sometimes for good, but generally for evil; at other times, they are seen merely as the projection by the child of internal dispositions. Initially, little account is taken of the influences of the years prior to the coming of self-consciousness and, even later, members of his family are termed mere "troublesome presences" (56) in his development. Furthermore, those figures of family or French history that the young boy came to admire are seen simply as "moving symbols through which I depict my whims" (49). By contrast the child is seen at other times as being totally formed by his environment. At the age of eight he says: "I was really nothing other than what they had made me" (93), and the importance of heredity is also recognized. Later he condemns his family for not "modeling his face" (42) in different fashion. The education system under which he grew up is blamed for its neglect of the body, while certain parts of the third section are a thoroughgoing condemnation of his society for its deficiencies and noxious influences.

Such conflicting statements merely reflect the difficulties of combining personal confession and social criticism through an analysis of a particular "self." Effective social criticism tends to cast the individual in the role of victim, while personal confession implies individual responsibility and guilt.

One of the most hateful characteristics of the self presented is, in the eyes of the narrator, its tendency to abstraction, to "become divorced from the world" (141). Consciousness of oneself as a distinct continuing personality is maintained as a definition of the human, but rejection of links with the world of concrete objects and the consequent retreat into the solitude of the self are castigated as a denial of life's creativity. In a bitter cry of anguish, which prefigures not only the closing words of *Le Feu follet* [Will-o'-the-Wisp] but also the *en soi–pour soi* ("in itself–for itself") tension in Sartre, little Cogle exclaims: "No, I have a horror of myself. What I want is not myself but the world. I want to touch things" (151). But at the age of sixteen he sees himself as totally determined by social forces as well as by an "inborn disposition" (141). This is the context of the recurring references to loneliness and solitude. Not only does the little boy choose to live "as alone as Robinson Crusoe" (70); he even sees the eyes of the other—be it dog or woman—as mirrors reflecting the unrelieved solitude of the individual. "Love is seeking solitude, furiously abandoning oneself to oneself, enclosing oneself in a prison, throwing the key through the bars" (39).

Escape from this self-centered prison is sought through the various enthusiasms that dot the pages of *Etat civil.* In a revealing comment in the first chapter of the book the narrator recognizes that patriotism is not for him an abstraction but a matter of achieving a degree of identity with other men. "I don't love [the French] so much because their genius is of such or such a nature, but because they are the men among whom I have lived" (19). Heroic ancestors are chosen as objects for admiration and enthusiasm even though the narrator is lucid enough to recognize that they come to assume the form his imagination desires. Boyhood enthusiasm for Napoleon in particular gives access to a world beyond the restrictions of the self: "I was emerging from myself, I was becoming aware of intoxication, dreaming, disorder" (42). The visit to Oxford in 1919, described in the next-to-last chapter of the book, fulfills much the same function. For one seeking liberation from self, family, and countrymen, the attractions of the foreign, both geographical and temporal, are obvious. Thus in Oxford, says the narrator, "far from my familiar quarters I discovered the truth of my soul" (174). Throughout Drieu's later writings this openness to the foreign as a possible source of salvation from intolerable restrictions reappears. As we have seen, it is already present in *Interrogation* and *Fond de cantine* in the form of the destructive but recreative barbarians from beyond the confines of European civilization.

In the last pages of *Etat civil* the contradictions caused by the attempt to combine personal confession with social criticism are resolved in the fashion that will become customary for Drieu and which we have already noted in the "Preamble" of *La Suite dans les idées*. The society in which little Cogle has been raised is invited to see in him one of its typical members with all its shortcomings and possibilities. Such a conclusion had been foreshadowed at the very beginning of the book by the representative name given to the boy, Cogle being the name given to the little Gallic rooster typifying France. It is not until toward the end of the book, however, that his representative function is stressed by his words: "I was sick, and it was the sickness of a whole people" (161).

Plainte contre inconnu

In the four short stories of *Plainte contre inconnu* [Complaint against Person Unknown, 1924] Drieu turns from the preoccupation with the self of *Etat civil* to present a wider vision of social life in the early postwar years. In the 1942 preface to *Gilles* he speaks of the best-known of the stories, "La Valise vide" [The Empty Suitcase], as "the detailed implacable analysis of a young man's character as it was formed by society and literature in 1920" (5), and the remaining three have a similar social emphasis. The stories focus on the reactions of a number of different individuals who find themselves with particular personal problems, but in each case both problems and reactions are seen largely as a function of the state of French society of the time. As the general title indicates, the complaint which the narrator feels impelled to make lacks specific direction. It simply expresses the disquiet of someone concerned about a situation in which the individual clearly has the role of victim, albeit a willing one. Although the memory of war and considerable nostalgia for the experience it made possible constitute a continuing background in each story, specific reference tends to fade as the young men depicted progressively adapt to a changed environment.

The first story, "Nous fûmes surpris" [We Were Taken by Surprise], takes the reader to the closing days of the war. It then describes the way in which Guy La Marche, a lieutenant in a tank corps, seeks to "improvise the peace" (13–14) which for him and his comrades-in-arms had come so unexpectedly.

As in all Drieu's works describing the situation of the demobilized soldier, the memory of the war experience in "Nous fûmes surpris" creates a sense of absence, a void, which Guy La Marche—and the narrator—desperately try to fill. Society, however, has not changed and offers nothing to occupy the soldier's initiative and latent strength. In consequence Guy La Marche drifts into the ambit of Parisian night life and succumbs to the cheap attractions that it offers.

That La Marche is recuperable and that he has not entirely lost a sense of the masculinity discovered in war are suggested by two brief incidents during the course of the story: the exaltation produced by a fast car ride with the narrator to Marseille; and a fight with the driver of a cart who had struck him with a whip. Such isolated incidents, trivial in themselves, show the narrator not only that there remains in La Marche "a vigorous but unusable quality" (29), but also that people like La Marche, who is clearly regarded as typical of a significant social group, are "not at their ease in the century" (32).

In "La Valise vide" one of the secondary characters of "Nous fûmes surpris," Gonzague, is subjected to close analysis. Like Guy La Marche he is a demobilized soldier lost in a society to which he frantically tries to adapt. With him, however, the war experience, such as it was, has faded and it is evoked only in the closing pages in an effort to explain the origin of certain of his current problems. The portrait that Drieu draws in this short story is certainly one of his most accomplished early pieces of writing and aroused considerable critical interest at the time of publication. It has obvious links with the character of Alain in *Le Feu follet,* written some seven years later. In all editions since 1963 *Le Feu follet* is in fact followed by the short essay *Adieu à Gonzague.*[2]

A "hollow man" with an "empty suitcase," Gonzague seeks to hide his inner void through constant hurried activity that makes it impossible for him to form deep friendships or achieve any degree of valid artistic appreciation. He shares with his contemporaries an obsession with what is new and changing, and like them lives in an only dimly recognized terror of being obliged to reveal the complete absence of firm values in his life. Solitude, with its threat of introspection, causes him constantly to seek company, even among his enemies, so that the abyss that time represents for him may be adequately filled.

Gonzague's lack of moral, spiritual, and intellectual "baggage" receives its clearest expression in his sexual behavior. In the environment of Paris he lacks the self-confidence to pursue to its conclusion any relationship with a woman, and he appears to the narrator to be constitutionally unable to play a typically male role in sexual affairs.

In his efforts to explain Gonzague's inadequacy in love, the narrator probes all aspects of his friend's life. Initially Gonzague admits to having a "physical problem," which remains unspecified but which makes him feel "abnormal, unclean, ridiculous, deprived of his rights over life" (52–53); he has had some involvement with drugs; he had had an unhappy love affair during the war; he had been briefly associated with a homosexual officer; and the influence of his father had prevented him from seeing front-line action. None of these elements, however, taken in isolation, adequately explains Gonzague's state, and the narrator is obliged to accept his friend's impatient remark: "When you have a new theory, you abandon all the others. You must not abandon any. I'm not so simple" (110). Hence the "illness" of Gonzague emerges as something the narrator is unable to explain fully except as a symptom of the society in which he lives. This is the belief that he expresses to his friend in the closing pages:

> But the erethism of our age is dogging you, disturbing you. You who are placid and yet ready to do a good day's work, you who are emininently normal, in a strange world of exasperated anguish-stricken individuals, you who have imagined that you are strange and under threat. Among so many sick people you have been unwilling to see yourself as healthy and you have seized upon some imaginary defect. (121)

By making Gonzague's "illness" both more pervasive and less specific than that of Guy La Marche, Drieu has, in "La Valise vide," not only created a character who is psychologically more convincing, but also established a closer link between personal psychology and social analysis. It is for this reason that the frequent remarks by the narrator on the state of society give the impression of valid commentary rather than questionable interpretation or even special pleading. In this manner Gonzague becomes a representative figure and a living condemnation of the society which Drieu felt moved to castigate.

In the third story, "Le Pique-nique" [The Picnic], Drieu passes from the analysis of a particular individual to the portrayal of a group of five, who spend a day on a deserted beach on the Mediterranean coast. The author's vision of this group is utterly depressing as he constructs a catalogue of promiscuity, homosexuality, and drug-taking, the result of a general superficiality that parades as a desire to savor any new experience that presents itself. The one exception is Liessies, whose idealism, firmly held despite his involvement with the group, sets him somewhat apart from the others and leads him to regard their furious mobility with abhorrence.

The specter of sterility hangs heavy over every aspect of the situation. It is reflected not only in the developing lesbian relationship between two of the characters but also in the shortness of the women's hair, their absence of adornment, and the vacuity of their conversation. The countryside through which the party passes on the way to the beach is such as to cause the human spirit to "contract to a barren idea" (127). For Liessies the very concept of "the human" seems threatened. This moral and physical aridity is highlighted by periodic indications of the possibilities latent in both people and countryside. Both elements are linked in one of the early images in the story when "to the vine prop clings opulent foliage covering fruit that are delicate, plentiful and compact like the tissues of a robust breast" (127). It is, however, in Gwen Brace's beauty that, for Liessies, the continuing possibility of life affirmation is chiefly found. Though surrounded by ugliness and "corroded by the ridiculous" (159), her beauty remains, like the grapes produced by the dry soil, a "fragile fruit" to suggest the persistence and wonder of life.

In "Le Pique-nique" references to war have almost completely disappeared, and with this absence comes greater authorial objectivity. Narration in the first person by one who is closely involved in the events described is replaced by the apparent objectivity of a third-person narrator not identifiably involved in the story (although it is clear that the character of Liessies tends to express the ideas and attitudes of the narrator in the first two stories). This impression of distance from the situation is accentuated by periodic changes of perspective as the author or Liessies attempts to assume the point of view of the "Creator" contemplating from afar "a fragment of the universe" (162) in which a rather pathetic group of individuals expresses its weak desires.

Third-person narration and consequent authorial distance are continued into the brief final story of the collection, "Anonymes" [Persons

Anonymous]. In this episode the development and decline of a love affair between two young people, Sue and Stan, is traced from the moment they first meet to their decision to marry. The title, as well as numerous comments scattered through the story, indicates that the situation of this couple is regarded as typical in modern society. At one point Stan is in fact baldly stated to be "one of us" (182).

As a statement of Drieu's highly conservative views on man-woman relationships, "Anonymes" is of considerable interest, but as a short story it is sadly lacking in technique. Authorial commentary, which frequently descends to downright moralizing, tends to obscure and even crush the account of the Sue-Stan relationship. The reader is informed not only of the couple's feelings and intentions but also of their mistakes and hidden desires, as for example in the following remarks about Sue: "Sue's desire was only dimly glimpsed. If its significance had been pointed out to her, she would have taken fright at seeing such an admission of weakness come from her" (185). Such remarks are often followed by generalizations applicable to the whole of society. At times, indeed, the work reads rather like a marriage-guidance manual. Although such faults of technique persist to some degree in Drieu's following novel, *L'Homme couvert de femmes* [The Man Covered with Women], they will gradually disappear as his powers as a prose writer develop.

L'Homme couvert de femmes

L'Homme couvert de femmes, which appeared in 1925, is the first of Drieu's novels to have the figure of Gille as its hero. The plot is exceedingly simple. Gille Gambier, en route to Biarritz from Paris, is invited by his friend Luc to spend a short period with him and his widowed sister Finette at their country home. During his stay, Gille is strongly attracted to Finette, but this does not prevent him from having several short-lived affairs with others at the villa. At a critical stage in his relationship with Finette he is reminded of his past life by the arrival of Jacqueline, with whom he had been associated during the war years. For a time he contemplates a lasting relationship with Finette but finally, despairing of its success, he leaves, distressed but free.

In *Le jeune Européen* Drieu states that his original intention in writing *L'Homme couvert de femmes* was to elucidate what he saw as a major social problem of his age: "I am going to show why nowadays a man and a woman don't get on together."[3] Although one may have doubts about the degree of Drieu's success in achieving this precise goal, it is clear that the interest of the work largely lies in this area. Frédéric Grover, for example, classifies the work as "a good document about the early 'twenties."[4] Through the tensions of Gille's personality and the portrayal of his friends and acquaintances, one has a view, albeit a very subjective one, of sexual attitudes among a section of the bourgeoisie that considered itself to be socially and morally liberated. Drieu himself felt that his sociological aim had been unduly obscured by an irrepressible tendency to allow personal problems and obsessions to intrude into his social analysis. As the young European recognized, however, the deepest probings of the self have considerable sociological significance. An excess of confessional outbursts by Gille may well be one of the major artistic faults of the work, but this ultimately increases rather than diminishes its social ramifications.

No sooner has Gille arrived than his attentions are sought by the motley array of Finette and Luc's guests and neighbors, and he finds himself in bed in quick succession with the simple, sensual Molly, and with Françoise, a Lady Chatterley–like figure whom he is pleased to picture as a "courageous and pure chatelaine" (29). He is, moreover, attracted by the strong Saxon figure of Lady Hyacinthia, who seeks to dominate her partners and express through them her energy and ambition. Although he is closely involved in the initiation and conclusion of these affairs, Gille is shocked by the apparent ease with which these women pass from one lover to another. The shared bed appears to establish no psychological or spiritual link for them, and their constant search for sensual pleasure degrades a function that Gille, despite his own conduct, strives to preserve at an ideal level. Shortly before his departure he reflects upon his recent experiences and passes this judgment:

> All of them follow the same harsh way of thinking, the same absurd watchword: live for the moment, ceaselessly and with untiring frenzy fulfill a function which, as a consequence of a fatal concurrence of the present conditions of the universe, has taken on for them enormous importance, and has assumed a majesty that is grotesque, at the very moment when they are reducing this function, along with the others, to its weakest resonance.
>
> Never have people lived a life that is so deprived. (209)

The contradictions of Gille's personality emerge through contact with such people. Molly calls forth the temptation of easy, irresponsible conquest designed to flatter the male ego and her invitation on the first night is instinctively accepted by the younger man. Yet in the midst of his egocentric and sensual reactions, Gille's enigmatic tendencies assert themselves. At one moment he finds himself looking beyond the imperfect individual before him and transposing the situation to an ideal level; at the next moment he allows reality to return to shatter his vision. There emerges a pattern of approach and withdrawal to which the reader becomes accustomed as the novel proceeds.

Gille's tendency to introduce idealistic elements into his personal relationships is regarded by most of the others with disbelief or cynicism, simply as a diverting role that he chooses to play. Luc, who brings the note of homosexuality into the novel, is at times inclined to place credence in his friend's sincerity, but at bottom he believes that there is little difference between Gille and those with whom he associates. "We are all like you" (191) is one of his final comments. He is attracted by his friend's high-flown theories of love but cannot believe that they are more than the airy nonsense of one who likes to play with words. His sister, however, sees rather more deeply, and instinctively recognizes in Gille "an outlaw who has subtly mingled with the crowd" (16). As such he has, she believes, close affinities with herself. It is also Finette who comes closest to discerning Gille's unwitting role as judge among his apparent peers. His moments of naive, idealistic enthusiasm in love call for a response from the others and serve to highlight the superficial, cynical lives they lead.

Paradoxically, perhaps, it is Gille's desire to bring Finette's latent idealism to the level of consciousness that accounts for their sexual fiasco. This incident, which closes the first part of the book and with it a whole chapter of Gille's life in this group, serves as a vivid symbol of the sterility of the group's attitudes. Through it the idealism that Gille seeks is seen as incompatible with the "liberated" but shallow ways of thinking that prevail. As long as Gille is able to approach his partners at the low level of their expectations, he proves sexually adequate. When, however, a deeper relationship of love is sought with one whose cynicism is merely an imposed role, a different range of values and a different life-style are demanded.

The second part of the novel, in which the relationship with Finette reaches an apparently successful stage only to be broken by Gille in a fit of despair, focuses particularly on Gille's past sexual history. As in *Le jeune Européen,* the origin of the conflict between "dream" and "reality" is situated in his upbringing, when the images and illusions conjured up by his reading were, he claims, not counterbalanced by contact with the physical realities of life. "My blood, lacking employment, was feeding a dream that became heavier and heavier, more and more monotonous, and which barred the way to tractable reality" (115). All his subsequent sexual problems are seen to stem from this disparity, as the vague visions of the ideal constantly intrude to destroy the acceptance and enjoyment of present realities. Gille feels powerless to prevent such intrusion since he cannot suppress the belief that the "two worlds" of dream and reality are linked. "[. . .] I know that they still maintain underground communications and I have not lost hope of pulling myself together, of blending all that" (121). Also from Gille's childhood and adolescence comes the familiar association of the mother image with the ideal, and this association, issuing in a dream of "pure nuptials" (120), further hinders his sexual adjustment. It is not without significance that the women with whom he associates in the novel are all older than his twenty-seven years and tend to be cast in a maternal role.

The possibility of the conjunction of dream and reality is evoked by the sudden arrival of Jacqueline and her husband. Jacqueline is the earliest example of what may be termed the "ideal" female figure in Drieu's fiction: the woman who is untouched by the degraded values of civilized life and whose motherly tenderness is accompanied by moral strength and frank sensuality. Gille recalls her as "that wonderful bell which contained all the sonorousness of which his soul was capable" (145). When he sees her again on this occasion he discovers that her memory had never left him.

The memories that Jacqueline's presence evokes come, predictably, to poison the imperfect reality of Gille's relationship with Finette. His romantic-mystical notion of a unique love relationship in life fills the final pages of the novel and arouses in him the disabused idealist's impatience for destruction. He is quick to seize on a number of pretexts to destroy the links with Finette that have gradually and naturally developed. Finette's inability to bear children, the result of an abortion in her youth, and her attachment to money are invoked by Gille to justify his rejection. In his moments of lucidity he recognizes these for the pretexts they are, but he nevertheless finds it impossible to resist in his life the destructive force of the ideal. He leaves the villa in a state of complete depression.

Pierre-Henri Simon noted in Drieu's writing what he termed "incurable Romanticism,"[5] and this characteristic emerges especially in the latter pages of *L'Homme couvert de femmes.* The fascination with the self, the impatience with the relative and the limited, and the quest for an elusive other-worldly ideal all proclaim Gille as a latter-day Romantic adrift in a cynical age. Drieu may have regretted the fact that his aim of social inquiry in fictional form had been obscured by the turbulent Romantic confession of the second half of the novel, but the two parts ultimately emerge as complementary. The first highlights the superficiality and sterility of the life led by those who are altogether lacking in idealism; the second half emphasizes the effects of Romantic idealism in rendering its victim incapable of adapting to reality at all. The fascinating character of Gille not only unites in his person these two extreme attitudes but also gives the novel its unity. Largely a literary transposition of a certain view of himself, Gille became for Drieu a fertile literary creation who, with his inner contradictions, reappears in later novels and short stories.

L'Homme couvert de femmes is Drieu's first attempt at the novel written in the third person and gives evidence of considerable experimentation in technique, particularly in the area of point of view. The single point of view of the autobiographical style of *Etat civil* is replaced by frequent sections of conversation, soliloquy, written communications, and by constant authorial comment. This change in style, the theoretical basis of which we have already examined in *Le jeune Européen,* creates, as in "Le Pique-nique" and "Anonymes," the impression of greater objectivity and serves Drieu's aim of social portrayal.

The work has many weaknesses, but not nearly so many as are claimed by those who, unduly influenced by the author's hasty disavowal of it in *Le jeune Européen,* would have us write the work off as worthless. Its defects are principally those that result from a writer's being unsure of his technique and hence self-conscious in his expression. There is, for example, as in "Anonymes," an unfortunate tendency to explain the significance of the words and actions of the characters, instead of allowing the reader to come to his own conclusions. Such literary paternalism falls heavily on a modern reader's ears.

This stylistic fault is, moreover, exacerbated by needless repetition in other ways, especially when Gille's confessional outbursts are recorded. There is also a certain periodic awkwardness in the transition from one point of view to another. This is most evident in the evocation of Gille's past: his need to communicate the view of his upbringing to Finette in writing seems rather artificial, as does the appearance of Jacqueline to arouse memories sleeping within him. These weaknesses are, however, simply indications of the writer's literary adolescence and will disappear from his later more confidently conceived and executed works.

Résumé

Considered together as Drieu's substantial literary production in the first half of the 1920s, *Etat civil, Plainte contre inconnu,* and *L'Homme couvert de femmes* provide a highly illuminating perspective on Drieu's search for an adequate literary vehicle to express his twin concerns: the nature of the self and the decadence of society. The opening words of *Etat civil* indicate clearly enough the writer's frustration: "I feel like recounting a story. Will I one day manage to recount something other than *my* story?" (7). Imprisoned by an obsession with the self that he feels bound to pursue, he is at the same time anxious to make valid literary contact with the outside world. We have seen how an attempt to achieve this contact is made in the final chapters of the work, but the principal preoccupation nevertheless remains that of the self. The first two stories of *Plainte contre inconnu* are also in the first person but they are narrated by one who seeks to introduce a certain objectivity into the presentation of a particular individual. Greater distance is achieved—though rather clumsily—in "Le Pique-nique" and "Anonymes" through the introduction of third-person narration and various other literary devices. Despite its faults, *L'Homme couvert de femmes* is an important watershed in Drieu's fiction in that the character of Gille emerges from Drieu's imagination to effect a reconciliation between individual analysis and social criticism. The fact that the two parts of the work, complementary though they are, remain relatively distinct in tone and emphasis, shows that the attempted reconciliation is imperfect. One has the impression, however, that Drieu's experimentation has brought him to a clearer conception of his literary goals and enabled him to discover appropriate literary tools.

Chapter Three
Individual Reactions to Decadence

Blèche

With *Blèche* (1928) Drieu emerges from self-conscious literary adolescence to reveal himself as a novelist of the first rank in the interwar period. The novel was greatly admired by Colette for the subtle variations of light and shade in its portrayal of human relations,[1] while the well-known *Nouvelle revue français* critic Ramon Fernandez, despite some reservations, found it to be a work of considerable interest in which there appeared the order, clarity, and unity that had previously been lacking in Drieu's writings.[2] Another critic of the time did not hesitate to describe Blèche as "one of the most delicate and authentic feminine figures that the modern novel has given us." Such contemporary praise does not, in retrospect, appear excessive since the depth of the psychological analysis and its tight structure make *Blèche* a model of the *roman d'analyse.*

As with *L'Homme couvert de femmes,* the plot is very slight. Blaquans, a conservative political journalist with *Le Catholique,* is given some valuable earrings by his wife, Marie-Laure, so that he may sell them and take a trip to America and Russia. They mysteriously disappear and, despite himself, Blaquans is led to suspect first his maid, Amélie, but then, with greater conviction, his secretary, Blèche. By the end of the novel the earrings are recovered but by this stage their loss has become quite incidental, interest having passed to the intricacies of the human relations that develop. Whereas the earrings are returned undamaged, and in fact have not been taken with any intent of theft, irreparable harm has been done on the human level, especially to Blaquans's relationship with Blèche. She attempts suicide, leaves the employ of *Le Catholique* and finally moves to a job in New York.

For Blaquans, the narrator and central character, the loss of the earrings precipitates an unpleasant process of self-discovery. Initially, the "theft" assumes importance not so much because of the financial loss it represents, but rather because it is seen as an assault on his integrity, as an outrage against the consideration that he feels is his due as a defender of the Church and other conservative social institutions. In his panic he pictures the thief as a mocking, scornful creature, deriding him from a position of psychological superiority. A mirror enables him to witness in himself a transformation of face and character that he senses as irreversible as he gradually becomes aware of the sordid world of human contact into which the event is forcing him. This is a world from which he has up till now successfully isolated himself. As for the characters of Sartre's *Huis Clos* [No Exit], Blaquans becomes acutely aware of the threatening presence of "the other."

On several occasions Drieu made reference to the political aspects of *Blèche,* and it is in these early pages that such an emphasis is most clearly visible. Blaquans, despite certain unusual aspects of his personal life, appears as a representative and defender of the bourgeois Establishment. He is labeled by the Left as "the most cunning and virulent agent of the forces of reaction" (15) and he is himself prepared to admit that all his journalism serves to "perpetuate the maxims of the old civilization of Paris" (15). Occupying such a role, he has come to expect a certain moral authority to be accorded to him and refusal of this becomes tantamount to an attack on the social forces that sustain him. The theft of the earrings, relatively trivial in itself, consequently takes on political overtones as Blaquans sees his whole way of life threatened. He pictures himself as a traveler in a train that is now out of control, flung "to the bottom of a ravine, wounded, abandoned" (21). The whole structure of his world has collapsed and he needs to reorient himself in completely strange territory.

Blaquans's reactions reveal the extreme fragility of the way of life he has chosen to lead. Prizing above all his solitude, he has isolated himself not just from normal social contact with his fellows but also from his wife and children, whom he visits only from time to time. The only people to penetrate the seclusion of his apartment in the Rue Chanoinesse are Amélie and Blèche, and a priest who is at present away in Rome. The intrusion of a threatening "other" brings such a carefully constructed edifice and comfortable isolation crumbling into ruins. Blaquans, suddenly a victim of "bourgeois bad conscience," finds himself obliged to reappraise his personal relationships. His suspicion of others invades the sterility of his environment and reveals to him how little the concepts of trust and fraternity really mean to him. Faced with such a condemnation he feels weak, "unclean" (25), and above all "unmasked" (25), one of the key words in his early self-analysis. He stands condemned by his own standards: "Cursed be he who casts the first stone" (24).

This is the background against which Blaquans's inquiry, occupying the first of the novel's three parts, proceeds. In turn he interviews Blèche and Amélie and finally has recourse to a distasteful private detective, Mordaque. Such contacts shed no light whatever on the disappearance of the earrings but merely serve to plunge Blaquans ever more deeply into his guilt-ridden world of suspicion. His visit to Mordaque is, in fact, an indication of his moral desperation. This individual, who, significantly, had occupied the Rue Chanoinesse apartment before Blaquans, assumes the function of a scapegoat. Charged with the suspicion that Blaquans finds intolerable, Mordaque clumsily pursues his investigations and leaves Blaquans free to reflect in relative tranquillity on the new light cast on his personal relations by the present events. Mordaque thus becomes, in terms of the novel's structure, a projection or objectification of Blaquans's "baseness" (219): this man, whose very livelihood is related to suspicion, represents those elements of personality which Blaquans is reluctant to confront. He is a living witness to Blaquans's "bad faith."

The other character to play an important symbolic role in the novel is Marie-Laure. Not once does she appear personally, but remains a shadowy, idealized figure, her purity counterbalancing the sordid world of the detective. As Mordaque is a projection of the seamier realities of Blaquans's life, so Marie-Laure stands as a symbol of the virginal purity, unsullied by contact with the baser facts of life, to which Blaquans aspires. Her absence from the stage of the novel is thus highly significant: she represents the willed absence of close human relations in Blaquans's life, the possibility of contact without commitment. At times one even wonders whether she has any greater reality than Blèche's "lover," who is mentioned from time to time but never appears and may well be a fabrication of Blèche's mind.

Like Jacqueline of *L'Homme couvert de femmes,* Marie-Laure had been met during wartime and her union with Blaquans had been sealed in that environment. "That girl whom I took, covered in the sweat and blood of men, anointed with a strong virile odor, gave me her soul and her body in one movement" (145). Now for Blaquans she presents the perfect conjunction of flesh and spirit, of the real and the ideal: she is the standard by which other women and other relationships are measured and found wanting. Vannier, the director of *Le Catholique,* sees this quite clearly when he says to Blaquans: "You don't love women, Blaquans, you are faithful to your own so that you can hate them all" (120). The figure of Marie-Laure is, in fact, largely a projection of Blaquans's refusal of responsibility and commitment to others except on his own terms. She is always described in images that portray passivity and dependence: as "a flame attached to its lamp" (118), as "deep transparent water" (119), or as "fine metal" (119) in the hand of her husband. She is the infinitely malleable, the infinitely reflective, the infinitely faithful, whose vision allows her husband to avoid the tensions and conflicts of normal social intercourse. This is the sense of his smug statement: "My secure love took delight in being a spectator of the world exterior to my wife and myself" (119). Her function as a projection of all that Blaquans desires is, moreover, confirmed by his admission: "I cultivated Marie-Laure's person like a second egoism and took pleasure in the situation, 'for,' I assured myself, 'my egoism, so deeply entwined with another, having doubled its roots, cannot now wither away'" (119).

Between these two personalized projections of Blaquans's egotistic ideal and the recently discovered baser aspects of his life lie the journalist's relationships with the two women who serve him in the isolation of the Rue Chanoinesse. Prior to the disappearance of the earrings, relationships had appeared to Blaquans to be straightforward, uncomplicated, and healthily impersonal, with each performing her particular function in such a manner as to respect his desire for strict privacy. Now, however, suspicion destroys these illusions of harmony. Blaquans is, moreover, forced to face not only the dark realities of his suspicions and their implications but also the reality of the jealousy and resentment between Amélie and Blèche. Both women, he discovers, have developed a possessive attitude toward him and resent the threats to their domination posed by the other. Indeed the disappearance of the earrings is a result of this mutual hostility, Amélie having removed them through fear of Blèche's intentions. The brief and reluctant inquiry that Blaquans conducts ineluctably leads him into close involvement with this abhorrent world of hostility, and he finds to his distress that his suspicion of Blèche has led him to descend to the level of being Amélie's accomplice in her efforts to vilify her rival. Under such circumstances an attitude of moral superiority is difficult to sustain. Parts II and III of *Blèche* may be seen as an effort by Blaquans to regain this isolated position of impersonal moral superiority where noble abstractions exclude the distasteful realities of human life.

In Blaquans's eyes, Blèche's crime is to have infiltrated his "moral life," to have disturbed the delicate equilibrium of his life shared between Marie-Laure and the Rue Chanoinesse. It takes very little to convince him that she had stolen the earrings through jealousy at Marie-Laure's initiative, and her offer to replace them with a pearl necklace is interpreted as an attempt to supplant her rival. In Part II of the novel Blaquans, having transferred to Mordaque the responsibility of pursuing the inquiry, reflects over the past twelve months of his association with Blèche in an effort to trace the path she has taken to make him so vulnerable. He is astonished to find that now her presence follows him into his solitude, disturbing his reflections on the great abstractions of his time "France, the Church, Communism" (91). His earlier impression that the present relationship of accuser and accused is the only human link that had ever existed between them is found to be false. He recognizes that he and Blèche had formed "a sort of couple" (155) and that the theft of the earrings could be seen as a logical consequence of this relationship, an effort by her to disturb the tranquillity of a situation which seeks to exclude the personal.

Blaquans's analysis of his personal relationships with Blèche shows him to be at a point of crisis where decisive action is necessary. He must either accept the reality of the relationship that has been allowed to develop and come to terms with it, with all the disruption to his personal life that this entails, or else retreat to his former isolation and destroy the one truly human contact that he has ever made. He chooses the latter course of action and destroys Blèche in the process. He sleeps with her, and it is this act which causes her to attempt suicide and finally go abroad, leaving Blaquans to his egotistical existence.

The third part of the novel, structurally similar in many respects to Part I, shows the successive steps taken by Blaquans to eliminate Blèche from his life and regain the appearance of moral superiority from which her emotional challenge has made him fall. The sexual encounter with Blèche, which is described in the first chapter, is treated with a mixture of delicacy and savagery which reflects the confusion of Blaquans's mind. Only half-conscious of his real motives in seeking her, he approaches her without desire, aware only of the conflict of pity and resentment that she inspires in him. As he takes her, pity yields its dominance to "incurable male resentment" (167) and the act which he had first imagined to be a conquest by Blèche—the ultimate penetration of his psychological defenses—becomes a weapon to destroy her. The consciousness grows that he has before him "a victim finally butchered" (169) and that sexual union under such conditions of mistrust, suspicion, and resentment has brought not union but irrevocable separation. Immediately after the sexual encounter he recognizes that he has made of her "a phantom that I was adapting to my feeble needs" (171). Blèche is thus made part of the restricted world of Blaquans's egoism.

The remainder of the novel is given over to Blaquans's attempt to reestablish himself in the eyes of Mordaque and Amélie. This he successfully achieves by implicating them both in Blèche's attempted suicide: Amélie for having taken the earrings and thereby casting suspicion on Blèche; Mordaque for having clumsily indicated to Blèche that she was under suspicion. The sexual act having been kept a close secret, Blaquans returns to his splendid, sterile isolation with his hands apparently unsullied.

A close analysis of *Blèche* reveals it to be a many-faceted work. It illuminates not only problems of man-woman relations at a particular social level, but also the more general question of commitment to the day-to-day issues of life rather than to the egotistical world of ideas "on their indestructible throne" (113). The challenge which Blèche presents to Blaquans's self-centered bourgeois intellectualism is simply one aspect of Drieu's dissatisfaction with the intellectual's attractive ivory tower in which he felt comfortably ill at ease. Already in the sexual embrace Blèche loses her personal identity to become "Woman" (167) and from this point on, as we have seen, she is incorporated into Blaquans's world. It is a significant indication of Drieu's attitude that such incorporation should be achieved through various acts of what Sartre was later to popularize as "bad faith." Moreover Blaquans's early recognition that he has no love of men and that concepts of fraternity mean nothing to him are never quite forgotten. From this point of view the novel represents a further stage in Drieu's reflections on the relationship between the "self" and the outside world. It is a stage that indicates a growing need for close personal and social involvement despite the continued attraction of abstract ideas. His subsequent work leans toward this theme of involvement.

Despite the use of first-person narration there is considerably greater objectivity in *Blèche* than in Drieu's previous fictional works. The adolescent, intensely personal cries of *Etat civil* and even of *L'Homme couvert de femmes* are replaced by the ironical distance of Drieu's presentation of Blaquans's "bad faith." For the first time one senses a personality behind the narrator fulfilling the function of Flaubert's ideal author, "present everywhere but visible nowhere." Such distance from the principal character is further accentuated by the portrayal of Blaquans's "bourgeois bad conscience" and the importance to him of moral respectability and authority. Blaquans is continually conscious of the eye of an unnamed "other" focused upon him, dictating his attitudes and actions. It is an "other" related more closely to appearances than to deep moral concern and as such creates an atmosphere of superficiality and insincerity that constitutes the book's most biting comment on the bourgeoisie.

Structurally the novel is one of Drieu's most carefully and successfully composed works. The structure of the narration takes, schematically, the form of a parabola. Part I illustrates Blaquans's "fall" from grace to the depths of suspicion and Part III (following the flashback that constitutes Part II) presents the ascent from the nadir of the sexual relationship to the prior immaculate heights of abstraction. There is, moreover, a nice symmetry between Parts I and III. Both begin with an important act and its consequence: in Part I the "theft" and Blaquans's suspicion; in Part III the sexual encounter and Blèche's suicide attempt. Moreover, in both there follow interviews between Blaquans and the other three parties to the drama.

Blèche is a work of considerable psychological and literary sophistication, much of its interest deriving from the moral ambiguities it contains. Blaquans's bad faith is motivated by a dimly sensed fidelity to intellectual objectivity, and to the world of ideas which both Blèche and presumably Marie-Laure recognize as valid. Moreover, Blaquans's betrayal of the three women in his life is to some degree counterbalanced by their assault on what is dearest to him: his solitude and independence. He betrays Marie-Laure's trust by sleeping with Blèche, but she, we learn, has invaded his privacy by asking Amélie to report to her on the situation at the Rue Chanoinesse; he betrays Amélie by partly blaming her for Blèche's suicide, but she is guilty of arousing his suspicion of Blèche by removing the earrings; he destroys Blèche by his suspicion and by sleeping with her, but it finally becomes clear that, although objectively innocent, she had intended to take the earrings herself. Such moral ambiguity, communicated in a work that is so technically brilliant, marks *Blèche* as a milestone in Drieu's literary career.

Une femme à sa fenêtre

Une femme à sa fenêtre [A Woman at her Window, 1929] is set in Greece in the early 1920s. A young Communist fugitive named Michel Boutros, responding to a tacit invitation, takes refuge in the Athens hotel room of French-born Margot Santorini, the wife of Rico, an Italian diplomat. Against a background of marital tension Margot persuades her husband to protect Michel and help him flee the country. A middle-aged French businessman, Raoul Malfosse, is prevailed upon by Margot, to whom he is sentimentally attracted, first to allow Michel to work as a mechanic at his villa and then to take him to Delphi, whence he is to proceed to Patras and freedom. During this time Margot becomes more and more drawn to the strong, tense Communist, whose pattern of life constitutes such an extreme contrast to the pointless existence led by the diplomatic circle in Athens. Michel is equally attracted to Margot but is reluctant to allow his feelings expression for fear that he will be led to betray and even abandon the harsh principles by which he lives. The environment of Delphi, however, makes him relent in his self-punishment: he sleeps with Margot and offers to take her with him, even though they both recognize the necessary fragility of such a relationship. Under pressure from Malfosse, Margot agrees to return to Athens before joining Michel at Patras, but it remains doubtful that this reunion will ever take place.

When he climbs into Margot's room on a May morning of 1924, Michel Boutros at once impresses her by his physical and moral strength. Initially he speaks to her in English—any connection with England is a sign of prestige in Drieu's characters—and his subsequent words and actions reveal him as a man who lives life with an intensity that communicates itself to others. He claims to have been implicated in the destruction of a factory at Salonica, a political act which immediately separates him from the valueless passive world to which Margot has grown accustomed and into which Rico has become integrated. For many years now his aim has been to find those areas of life that retain the strength and energy that alone he respects: "What he had been thirsting for since the puberty of his spirit was to lay hold of the movements of energy across the world in their moment of essential life; he needed to have the closest contact with the forces that were dominant at the moment in which he was living" (218).

Boutros's commitment to communism is explained in terms of this quest for energy and life. Devoid of genuine ideological convictions, he has given himself to that movement which provides clearest evidence of a vigor and vitality that will challenge and perhaps destroy the decadent West. "I couldn't care less about doctrine and all its pretentious little details" (245), he cries to Malfosse, and he remains fully conscious that he is both using and being used by a movement that bids fair to satisfy his psychological needs. Boutros has consequently the psychology of an adventurer and to this extent has certain affinities with the early heroes of André Malraux such as Garine in *Les Conquérants* [The Conquerors], a work which appeared several years earlier and which Drieu greatly admired.

The tensions and paradoxes of Boutros's personality first reveal themselves in his physical appearance. Margot notes his "delicate roughness" (33), an impression communicated both by his hands, which, despite their hairy, muscular appearance, are "supple, fine" (33), and by his clothing, which is rough and worn out but shows evidence of taste. He has, for Margot, a personality that has undeniable "grace" but there is about him an austerity and severity that destroy any trace of sophistication. The enigma that he presents also to Rico and Malfosse is indicated by the contradictory qualities they discover in him: he is both "cunning and sensitive, devious and straightforward, passionate and skeptical" (110). It is Margot who first interprets these surface contradictions and sees in them evidence of deep psychological conflict: "He wasn't from the working class, he was from the bourgeoisie, with complicated perhaps illusory motives. She sensed in him a world of contradictions, of torments, which had been overcome, but which were not quite stifled" (93). Boutros's conflict is internal rather than with society. As he himself later explains to Margot: "It is easier to produce a revolution in the street than in people's hearts" (190).

The revolution that Boutros seeks to accomplish within himself is the suppression of all those elements that he associates with the money and comfort-oriented Western bourgeoisie. In particular he shuns all contact with women, who represent for him "money, luxury, softness, peace" (186). Indissolubly bound to the dying society whose destruction he sees as a desirable necessity in the cycle of history, women are a temptation to abandon his activism. Consequently, despite his attraction to Margot, Boutros regards her as an enemy, not just because of the class to which she belongs, but simply because she is a woman.

As with all Drieu's novels of this period it is principally in the crucible of man-woman relationships that ideas are tested, tensions revealed, and an adequate philosophy of life sought. At Delphi, where in antiquity the deep secrets of the earth were communicated through woman, Boutros sees with distressing clarity the fundamental contradictions of his attitude of misogyny. How can he, who claims to be seeking the deeper aspects of life, deny himself the means of access to them? A prey to the awesome spirituality of the site, and keenly aware of this connection with the "divine recesses of the universe" (210) through woman, Boutros's mistrust of woman fades and, in a period of intense lyrical optimism, he experiences sexual communion with Margot that creates a sense of the union of the "two halves of the universe" (226).

Despite its spiritual intensity the experience is shortlived and the problems of daily realities, represented first by the interruption of Malfosse, come flooding back. Drieu himself, sensing that his lyrical flights have carried him too far, reminds us in a rather clumsy authorial intervention that Margot is possibly pregnant and that sexual passion brings in its train "all those things that are heaviest, most far-reaching and most mundane in their consequences: children and sickness, family and old age" (229). Access to the absolute serves to give even greater prominence to the restrictions and frustrations of normal living. Michel departs for an uncertain future with the lessons of Delphi weighing heavily upon him.

During his few days at Athens and Delphi, Michel Boutros comes into contact with only three people, but in each he provokes a crisis of self-awareness. Malfosse comes to recognize the poverty of a life given over to the production of wealth. Devoid of ideas, and hence with little real hold on life, he sees how little he has to offer a woman like Margot. The intensely human values of Boutros make money lose its worth. Even Rico, the handsome and cynical "melancholic Don Juan" (79) who tries to lose himself in his world of women, responds momentarily to the challenge of Boutros's masculine power. He is sufficiently perceptive to find fundamental resemblances between himself and Boutros and sees in the Communist the man he might have been had he not chosen to cultivate the more superficial aspects of his personality. Despite this insight he lapses back into his customary ways and almost completely disappears from the stage of the novel. The response of his wife Margot, however, is of quite a different order.

The emptiness of Margot's life and the possibilities of satisfaction that Boutros offers are presented through the striking imagery of the early pages of the novel. Distractedly standing at the window of her hotel room as night yields to day, Margot senses in the scene outside a reflection of her own inner emptiness: "That street and all those that follow on from it, that whole labyrinth emerging from the shadows exists only in the eyes of the solitary observer: it is an inner reality that he traverses in his dream" (20). The sun with its "illusion of salvation and triumph" (19) has not yet appeared and in any case will pass unnoticed by the town's inhabitants still rapt in their slumbers. Only Margot is awake. Having abandoned the facade she presents to society as a diplomat's wife, she stands psychologically open and ready to receive the masculine force of the sun in the form of the Communist fugitive.

The symbolic identification of Michel Boutros with the sun (which reaches a climax at the time of sexual union when "the huge blacksmith on the horizon was beating an iron bar at white heat" [224]), does not obscure Margot's role in inducing self-awareness in him and satisfying the psychological needs that he has repressed. There is in fact throughout the novel a complementary relationship between these two characters which receives its ultimate and clearest expression in the sexual encounter. Like Drieu's other idealized women characters, Margot was a nurse in wartime, and it is in this "maternal" role of one who brings tenderness, solace, and refuge that she is frequently cast. The haven of her room makes Boutros dependent upon her at the outset, and it is significant that he should note in her at this early stage "something firm and maternal" (30). She in her turn is reminded by him of "the wounded soldiers that she had tended in former years with their air of children bracing themselves" (28). Later, in the sexual embrace, Boutros is led to consider her as a "wonderful refuge" (231) that offers him "the freedom of Eden" (233).

That Boutros and Margot are basically complementary and even interdependent is suggested at the level of symbol by the fact that while Boutros is associated with the sun, Margot is seen in terms of light. When Boutros first sees her he is dazzled by the radiance of her body: "All that flesh was light, but what an exceedingly insinuating light it was, one that would not have been produced by the lightest oil in the most delicate alabaster vase. That whole slender form, bathed in a single ray" (27). This vision of light accompanies Margot through the novel until its natural link with the sun is achieved in the final pages.

Drieu's novels dealing with man-woman relationships tend to finish on a relatively pessimistic note, with decadent society seen as being at least indirectly responsible for the impossibility of sexual satisfaction and harmony. The pessimism in this novel, however, goes much deeper than this social level and reveals a fundamentally tragic view of human life.

There are many expressions of this view of life but, ironically, it is from Malfosse that its clearest expression comes. Speaking to Boutros he says: "In life we are never more threatened than when we yield to the strongest impulse of our heart" (243). Though the words have quite a different meaning for Malfosse than they do for Boutros, they provide a telling commentary on the relationship between Margot and Boutros, which has shortly before reached its climax. Even in the absence of social constraints Michel recognizes that there is an inherent contradiction in man's relationship with woman, a contradiction which, in dialectic fashion, grows with the intensity of the relationship: "At that moment he bravely acknowledged this two-fold aspect of woman, he recognized that a man cannot become aware of what is heaviest in the heart of destiny unless he accepts Woman. And to accept Woman, he must take a woman. Now he would have in his arms all the earthly weight that a man can bear: the crowd and woman" (240). His relationship with Margot has brought him to the "essence" of life, but only to discover an unresolvable tension, an example of what Camus was later to call "the absurd." His final thought, shared by Margot, that their best hope lies in transforming love into the more durable relationship of friendship, is clearly an admission of defeat and not, as more than one critic has seen, a sign of hope.[3]

Apart from illuminating and developing these aspects of man-woman relationships, *Une femme à sa fenêtre* pursues the reflections of earlier works on the nature of the self and its links with external reality. Expression is given to an interesting view of the duality of the self, one that recalls the ideas of Proust. It is clearly expressed by Boutros when he says: "A man has two selves: the first is narrow and superficial, and isolates him from the world; the other is subterranean and radical, and unites him to the world" (125). The pattern of life of the three main characters may in fact be interpreted as a function of their awareness of this duality and their response to it.

Like the young soldier of *Interrogation,* Rico had in wartime experienced something of life's intensity. He had lived at a profounder level than he finds possible in peacetime and it is the "void left by grandeur now absent" (130) which drives him to bury himself in his erotic pursuits. Haunted by the possibilities of self-fulfillment he had glimpsed in war, and consequently dissatisfied with the society in which he moves, Rico has chosen to "destroy women and to destroy himself through women" (130), "to deny himself and destroy himself" (72), "to forget himself, destroy himself" (124).

Boutros is, as we have seen, also engaged in a process of self-repression, but of the narrow, superficial self which he associates with bourgeois society. He too is fearful of women but for precisely the opposite reason to Rico's. It is another of the novel's ironies that association with Margot should bring Boutros to see the justice of Rico's fears of woman, namely that they present a challenge to develop the other self which has roots in the earth. It is also of particular significance that in the "Eden" of Boutros's perfect sexual union all self-awareness is lost.

Margot presents yet another reaction to the problem of the duality of the self. Avoiding the extreme attitudes of her husband and Boutros, she accepts the superficiality of her social environment, but in her relationships guards a certain distance that makes her somewhat of an enigma to her friends. Instinctively aware that there is a side of her personality that needs to be protected, she adopts an attitude of coquetry which for her is "a way of creating a stage setting around oneself in which one's dream finds refuge" (80). It is to the preservation of this dream, this dimly glimpsed subterranean self, that Boutros refers when he notes his impression that Margot, despite all her sentimental disappointments, "had preserved herself" (182). The coming of Boutros brings reality to Margot's dreams, the disappearance of her coquetry, and a clearer consciousness of the duality of her nature.

The setting of the novel in Greece allows Drieu to illustrate and develop within the structure of a fictional narrative his ideas on the birth and decay of civilizations. The Acropolis with its ruins is a reminder of the fate of all civilizations and it is significant that it should give its name to the hotel in which the diplomats from all the countries of the West gather. They and the countries they represent hang under the same condemnation and are even now as sterile and dead as the ruins they slavishly admire. The spirit that inspired the Parthenon has now passed to other lands and other societies, and it is among these that Boutros prefers to work: "'What you call beauty,'" he exclaims to Malfosse, "'is life that is dead'" (153).

The trip to Delphi, although undertaken for very practical reasons, becomes a pilgrimage to the sources of the spirit that inspired the building of the Parthenon, which is found still to retain its ancient power. As the aridity of the present-day Acropolis shows the old age and death of a civilization that has lost touch with nature, so the forests, hills, and clefts of Delphi tell of the creative forces of life that remain available to man. In this environment Malfosse loses his assurance while his two companions discover an inner unity that has links with nature. Such unity is foreshadowed by the description of the countryside as they approach Delphi: "Boutros [. . .] did not fail to marvel at this sudden display, at this clever terracing with its elements intermingled: plain, sea, mountain, sky. Delicately sewn to the lines of the mountain crests, the sky does not dominate this setting: it is attached to it and preserves its place in the pattern of the other natural wonders" (146).

In most respects *Une femme à sa fenêtre* is a more ambitious novel than those that preceded it and indicates Drieu's growing confidence in his literary talents. Although not really complex, the plot has considerable intrinsic interest and shows the author to be reaching beyond the earlier narrowly psychological studies and developing the abilities that will lead to the "polyphonic novels of the later 1930s. An indication of the general attractiveness of the work is in fact that it was translated into English and Czech as early as 1931, and that in more recent times it has served as the basis for a feature length film. It is, furthermore, the first of Drieu's works in which the setting is outside France. In his artistic efforts Drieu is obviously trying to break out of the restrictive circle of an inward-looking society. In this way his literary imagination runs parallel to the development of his concept of the self.

The work is structurally similar to *L'Homme couvert de femmes*. Two almost exactly equal parts of six chapters, the one centered on Athens, the other on Delphi, are divided by a central chapter in which a significant crisis of self awareness takes place. Ideas are, however, much better incorporated into this framework than in the earlier very self-conscious work. The same tendencies to lyrical flights of a mystical nature are present but they lose their earlier vague, abstract quality by being related to the precise historical and religious associations of Delphi. It is true that a certain self-consciousness remains in the form of periodic clumsy authorial interventions, but these rarely disturb the natural flow of story and ideas.

Stylistically, *Une femme à sa fenêtre* is marked by the growing use of symbolism, particularly related to nature. As we have seen, sun and light are associated with the two main characters, and the whole natural environment of Delphi is evocative in the extreme. This development in Drieu's expression is, of course, related to his lyricomystical preoccupations. It goes, however, rather further than this and shows a desire to escape the dangers of abstract pseudophilosophical expression and to set his ideas in a framework of concrete, if symbolic, reality.

Le Feu follet

Le Feu follet (1931), one of Drieu's most somber novels, recounts the last day in the life of Alain, a thirty-year-old drug addict, as he visits acquaintances and friends in an effort to discover a valid reason for not putting an end to his life. Lydia, a rich American woman with whom he is found in the opening pages, has little else to offer him than money: it is with the 10,000 francs she gives him that he is enabled to make his way from one depressing situation to another. His first stop is at the rest home where he is undergoing treatment for his addiction from a Dr. de la Barbinais. More of a fearful businessman than a physician, Barbinais presides over a sorry collection of patients, among whom Alain appears full of initiative for having recently dared to leave the clinic without permission. It is evident that Alain can expect no help from such a lifeless group and from a doctor whose main treatment seems to be a shallow optimism that lacks personal conviction.

After a few desultory efforts to find inspiration in writing, Alain goes for lunch to the home of a companion of his youth, Dubourg, who has largely withdrawn from social contact to engross himself in his obsession of Egyptology. With his quiet submissive wife and children he leads an existence which Alain sees as a "dull, slow death" (102). Although Dubourg understands Alain's problems perhaps better than anyone else, he ultimately proves incapable of crucial encounter. Alain takes heroin in the studio of Falet, a photographer, and under the effects of the drug the pace of his life briefly quickens. He spends some time with two acquaintances, Praline and Urcel, who attempt to justify their opium smoking by the idea of the risk, and hence the intensity of life, that it brings. Unconvinced, and indeed scornful of the way they are deluding themselves, Alain goes for dinner to the house of Cyrille and Solange Lavaux, whose guests include a number of people who have achieved a high degree of social success. In particular Alain meets a brutish adventurer, Marc Brancion, but his attempts at conversation with him pass from the ridiculous to the grotesque. Solange Lavaux alone has sufficient sensitivity to see that she may be able to restore Alain's faith in life. Alain, however, aware of her much greater attraction to the forceful masculinity of Brancion, leaves the group, and, after a phone call from her the next morning, shoots himself.

Drieu's choice of title for the novel is particularly appropriate. The association of will-o'-the-wisp with decay and death gives a vivid image of Alain's wan life and of the attitudes of those he frequents. As Frédéric Grover vividly puts it, Alain is the "emanation of a rotting society."[4] Perhaps of greater consequence for the novel is the image that the title evokes of insubstantiality, of transitory form and momentary intensity without sustaining power. This is essentially the sort of life Alain leads and is certainly descriptive of his inability to put down roots in any part of the social structure. It is probably also a fair description of the inner personality of Alain and his fellows, but this question is not finally resolved and remains one of the novel's attractive ambiguities.

In the very first chapter Alain is described as a "hollow phantom" with a "mask of wax" (15) and this image, recalling Gonzague's "empty suitcase," accompanies him through his peregrinations. Anxious at all times to please, and in general successful in attracting the interest and affection of men and especially women, Alain is incapable of pursuing personal relationships to the stage of deep love or friendship. He communicates "a feeling of absence" (60) which disconcerts others, causing them to turn from him to pursue those solid realities of the world that are for them "guarantees of existence" (60). Lydia takes fright at her gentle lover's involuntary indifference and flees back to America, where men are seen to be hard and brutal, but real. For the moment she finds her reality in the money which she passes to him and which she senses is for him more a psychological than a financial need. Dubourg is first distressed, then angered, to find that Alain's personality and problems deny precise definition. He fumbles in the dim half-light of Alain's world, trying to locate the source of his friend's despair to discover a "secret raison d'être" (90) that may develop and bring consistency to Alain's life. But his hands find only the air as the flame flits elsewhere. Praline and Urcel try to induce Alain to establish a sense of identity on his drug addiction and to accept this fact as the one positive element in his life. However, he rejects the "fraternity of risk" that his friends claim to constitute, is in turn rejected by them, and prefers the lucid and lonely uncertainty of the night and the empty street. His encounter with Brancion confirms the sense of inner emptiness and drives him to his final positive act.

Alain's deficiencies are presented by Drieu and felt by Alain himself as a fundamental inability to make contact with "things." "That's the way it is, I can't put out my hand, I can't touch things," Alain blurts out to Brancion in a vain effort to gain attention and sympathy. "In any case, when I touch things, I don't feel anything" (152). His sense of isolation and restriction is vividly conveyed by the description of his room at the rest home. By attracting such epithets as "with no way out," "eternal," and "ideal prison" (32) it takes on the most general connotations and is not without recalling the situation in Sartre's *Huis Clos:* "His self, hollowed out, was there, like a smaller box in a bigger box. A mirror, a window, a door. The door and the window opened out on to nothing. The mirror opened out only on to himself" (32). In such a situation he is restricted to the role of Narcissus, his eyes fixed on his image in the "calm water" (58) of the mirror.

It is for reasons of this order that the Lavaux household is so attractive to him. The simple, solid stone house with its inhabitants who are resolved to accept life "firmly and frankly" (141) represents everything to which he aspires. Here the beautiful Solange reigns like "a princess to whom the social upstarts haven't yet taught arrogance" (141); her husband has both the money and the sexual prowess that Alain envies; and Brancion has the assurance of a cinema hero. "In this house, I am exactly in the situation in which I would like to have lived, in which I ought to have triumphed" (147), Alain confides to himself. But finally he beats an ignominious retreat, disillusioned and patently unable to link this dream world with the reality of his feeble self.

This discrepancy that Alain finds between dream and reality frequently develops into a contrast between form and substance and is a feature of every description presented from Alain's point of view: "For him the world was peopled with nothing but empty shapes" (109). As he watches Lydia dress in the dreary hotel room, the undeniable beauty of her face and body fades before other impressions. Her face takes on the anonymity of a mask to present "a strange caricature of life" (15) and her skin resembles the leather of a luxurious but empty suitcase. The house of Dubourg, whose invitation to lunch he had accepted with a pleasure born of hope, appears to Alain as he mounts the stairs to be an "old carcass" which has been "gnawed to the bones" (75) by human habitation. The activity of Falet, moreover, in which appearance and reality might reasonably be expected to achieve some point of contact, is in fact essentially an art of deception.

The distinction made in the novel between "things" and "objects" suggests that the former have for Alain a very general sense and are seen primarily as other beings with whom a personal relationship is sought. "Objects," on the other hand, have consistency, solidity, and hence reality, and, while immensely attractive, remain impervious to the presence of "the other." During the course of the novel Alain is progressively reduced to this world of hard, substantial objects by the gradually narrowing circle that he feels about him. The sense of this restriction is indicated by the fact that the novel opens with a description of the closest of human relationships and closes with the entry of an object into the seat of human affections: "[. . .] one knows where one's heart is. A revolver is solid, it's made of steel. It's an object. Finally make contact with the object" (178). In Alain's life the impersonal world of the object is ultimately the only one through which some sense of reality can be achieved.

The importance that sexual relationships assume in the novel illustrates Drieu's conviction that they provide the best measure of psychological and social health. In an article written two years after the composition of *Le Feu follet,* Drieu states this quite unequivocally: "Man primarily expresses his freshness or his barrenness, his good or poor health, his simplicity or his complexity, his rectitude or his deviousness in his amorous behavior."[5] Alain's sickness is seen and experienced primarily in this way. It is no accident that the train of events in the novel passes from a sexual relationship that leaves both parties unsatisfied to one that is dimly projected but never eventuates. Moreover, Alain sees the reasons for his drug addiction in terms of sexual incapacity. "But I take drugs, because I make love poorly" (95), he confides to Dubourg.

The dismal scene with Lydia in the first chapter sets the tone and establishes the pattern for the reactions of Alain in the rest of the novel. As on previous occasions, sexual contact does not bring the desperately hoped for illumination of his own personality or that of his partner: each experiences the "truncated reality" (9) of the other. Such repeated failure demonstrates to Alain his lack of control over women and through them over life itself. As in *Une femme à sa fenêtre,* woman is sensed as being the path to the depths of the real.

Alain's idealization of woman has, however, elements which serve to distinguish him quite clearly from the hero of *Une femme à sa fenêtre.* Whereas the association of woman and money—a constant of Drieu's writing—is the source of Boutros's misogyny, for Alain it is at least to some degree what makes woman so desirable. Dubourg suggests to Alain that it is precisely this association which spoils his sexual relationships, and the truth of this statement is not denied by his friend. Woman thus becomes "both the object desired and the source of emasculation that destroys desire."[6]

Alain's attraction to money is, however, a phenomenon of greater complexity than is at first apparent. As Lydia recognizes, his need of money is fundamentally psychological. He is obsessed by the sight of her check for 10,000 francs, not because of a base worship of Mammon, but because of its capacity to communicate power to his existence: "He was totally absorbed in contemplating this rectangle of paper, charged with power" (35). Through it he hopes to come into close contact with life, to live more intensely, Dubourg glimpses this truth when he says to Alain: "In your imagination money has an importance that is out of proportion to your real liking for it" (85). More than a "fetish" (34), money becomes a myth through which man's relationship with the world is construed. It is for this reason that his need to "burn up banknotes" (116) has grown from year to year as his hold on reality becomes more tenuous. Furthermore, it is significant that those men whom Alain envies because of their strength and initiative tend to be pictured with their pockets bulging with money.

Social criticism in *Le Feu follet* is perhaps most apparent at this level of money as myth. Dubourg analyzes Alain's inability to adapt to society in terms of social origins (84), but his friend's impatience indicates that for him the phenomenon goes rather deeper than this. Several of the author's remarks tend to confirm this. Alain's attitudes and actions, epitomized by his addiction, are seen as having positive value in that they are an implicit rejection of a society based on money. Once again it is Dubourg who first proposes this idea:

> Perhaps there was a great deal of life in this refusal of life by Alain? It was for him a way of denying and condemning not life itself, but the aspects of it that he hated. [. . .] Drug addicts are mystics in a materialist age who, no longer having the strength to breathe life into things and to sublimate them to the level of symbol, undertake the opposite task of reduction, and wear and chip away at them until they reach in them a kernel of nothingness. (93)

Alain, like most of Drieu's heroes, thus becomes both victim and accuser, the blade and the wound, the nihilist in search of the absolute.

In a way that has striking resemblances with Camus's treatment of Meursault in *L'Etranger* [The Outsider], Drieu uses Alain's lucidity and honesty as a further means of social criticism. On several occasions Alain destroys, with the implacable honesty of instinct, the illusions that his friends conjure up to give meaning or justification to their own lives and also to his. In his rejection of Dubourg's invitation to adopt "another personality" that will aid his integration into society, Alain shows that he retains a concept of his self to which instinctively he wishes to remain faithful. He demands, indeed, that he should be accepted as he is and that any help should respect his individuality. Angered by Urcel's hypocrisy, he mutters: "I know only myself. Life is me" (130), and he prefers to die rather than betray the one certainty that he still has. One is reminded of Meursault's reaction to the chaplain in prison. In this respect, Alain, despite the antiheroic tendencies he shares with Meursault, also becomes a hero whose very existence constitutes a challenge to social and intellectual norms. *Le Feu follet* is, as Frédéric Grover remarked in 1978, a novel which still frightens.[7]

Despite the extreme rapidity with which Drieu claims to have written *Le Feu follet,* the novel gives every indication of careful construction and considerable attention to detail. The structural patterns are of particular interest. From one point of view the development is quite linear: Alain passes from one person or group to another in a simple progression that culminates in his death. Concomitant with this linear approach, however, is the sense of circularity that is conveyed as Alain feels the world closing in upon him to reduce relationships to that of the self and the object.

A third pattern, which relates the work structurally to *Une femme à sa fenêtre,* has as its center the crucial interview with Dubourg. Up to this point Alain's encounters serve to illuminate his present state mainly by reference to his past history. Following this interview, however, hope fades and Alain's life continues in a moral descent to oblivion. Drieu's ability to combine these geometrically diverse patterns into a coherent, impressive whole shows the degree to which his literary powers have developed.

Possibly Drieu's most impressive achievement in *Le Feu follet* is his creation of an atmosphere of moral and psychological ambiguity. Alain is a much more complex character than his literary brothers of prior novels. As we have seen, his personality resists the simplistic efforts made by Dubourg to reduce it entirely to psychological categories, since it enshrines the conflicts and contradictions of a whole society. The novel reflects this complexity in many ways, but notably in its imagery, which is dominated by concepts of hollowness and emptiness and by the indeterminate color of gray. Alain's world is one of false facades and empty, depressing streets, and he moves constantly in a deceptive half-light:

> It was November, but it wasn't very cold. Daylight was slipping over night like a wet cloth over a dirty floor. They walked down la rue Blanche, between the garbage tins, filled with offerings. Lydia was walking ahead, tall, square shoulders, on ankles of clay. In the gray light of dawn her makeup formed, now here now there, a feverish blemish. (17–18)

Psychological and moral complexity is also communicated by the use of point of view. It is, of course, Alain's point of view that is dominant in the novel but the attitudes of a multitude of minor individuals toward him are also presented. Authorial comment is frequent, but it tends to be less direct and is often incorporated almost imperceptibly into the flow of Alain's ideas to produce a sense of uncertainty corresponding to the ambiguities of Alain's drugged world.

Résumé

Drieu's three works of fiction of the period 1928 to 1931 present an interesting and illuminating examination of a series of individual reactions to a particular social situation. *Blèche, Une femme à sa fenêtre,* and *Le Feu follet* all illustrate the tendency that we have noted in Drieu to present social criticism through the analysis of a particular individual, but in each of these novels the individual depicted has his own distinctive characteristics and is seen as representative of a particular social grouping. Blaquans is a member of the conservative, religiously oriented bourgeoisie. He seeks to maintain the status quo in his own life and in his society even though this involves him in "bad faith." Boutros, on the contrary, has taken a revolutionary stance and suppresses personal problems by attacking the Establishment and by seeking those areas of life which retain some vigor. Alain represents those who are largely victims of the social order. Unable to find the initiative of a Boutros and unwilling to embrace the "bad faith" of a Blaquans, Alain allows himself to drift in an indifferent environment to an encounter with death.

Viewed in this way the novels form an interesting trilogy in which Drieu not only examines society from three quite different vantage points but also analyzes three possible reactions by the self to the situation that confronts it. In each case the internal divisions of the self are stressed and greater self-awareness is provoked by the situation that develops, but at the same time these individual problems serve to elucidate social hypocrisy and indifference. This combination of individual psychological analysis and social criticism, present in all three, receives its clearest yet most subtle expression in *Le Feu follet.*

A further important feature of these three novels is the increasing authorial objectivity that manifests itself. Careful use of narrative technique, point of view, and authorial intervention enables Drieu to objectify the "self" presented and to achieve a tone of involvement without close identification. Furthermore, the periodic suggestions, especially in *Une femme à sa fenêtre,* that the human condition is of its essence tragic, indicate a widening of perspective and a progression from the particular to the general that will develop further in his works of the late 1930s and 1940s.

Chapter Four
The Quest for Intensity

Drôle de voyage

With *Drôle de voyage* [Strange Journey, 1933] Drieu returns to an analysis of the character of Gille, who had appeared in *L'Homme couvert de femmes* some eight years before. Certain commentators have in fact seen *Drôle de voyage* as merely a successful rewriting of the earlier relatively immature work and it is true that there are certain features that the two novels share. Gille, the central character of both, pays court to a woman closely linked to a decadent environment and social structure. He is led to consider marriage but he finally flees the situation, having convinced himself that it would be impossible to separate this woman from the values and attitudes that her social environment leads her to adopt.

Once these general resemblances of central character and plot are recognized, however, it becomes clear that *Drôle de voyage,* despite its relatively simple structural framework, is a novel of much greater complexity. It has ramifications that extend beyond social comment to a profound questioning of the individual's situation in the world and of his very identity. Frédéric Grover notes that *Drôle de voyage* is "broader in its implications" than the first Gille novel, and he goes on to say: "We are not shown only the face Narcissus sees in the mirror of the water; we see Narcissus meditating on the mystery of his inner contradictions."[1] It is this fact, together with its vastly improved literary technique, that makes the work of particular significance in Drieu's development as a writer and a landmark in the exploration of the "self."

The broad implications of *Drôle de voyage* may be seen most clearly through an examination of the concept of the "journey" contained in the title. At its simplest level the journey refers to Gille's travels in France and Spain. Initially he is found in "La Béraude," a country house in the Pyrenees, with his friends Yves, Baptiste, and Gabriel Cahen-Ducasse and their stepmother. He is attracted by Béatrix, the daughter of some English aristocrat visitors, and shortly after their departure he follows them to their home in Granada. From here he returns to his employment—and a new mistress—in Paris, only to travel back to Granada several months later with the intention of marrying Béatrix. Speedily convinced of the long-term disaster of such a union, he leaves precipitately to pursue his travels elsewhere.

The preoccupation of the novel with decadence suggests that the journey may also be seen as one taken through a society whose values are refused. "La Béraude," Granada, and Paris are seen in turn as infected by the same modern disease which saps all human creative capacities and hence disrupts personal relationships. From time to time this journey through a society in decay is viewed in even more general terms as man's journey through life itself. Indeed the title is used in this sense in the text of the novel when Gille muses aloud to Béatrix: "[. . .] if a woman were willing to give herself with me to this strange movement of the world, if a woman were willing with me to treat with equal irony and detachment and tenderness everything that one sees during this strange journey, we could take our seats beside each other . . ." (146).

The most significant aspect of the journey taken by Gille, whether it is considered on the literal or the figurative level, is that it constitutes a process of self-discovery. His experiences in the different settings of the novel and especially in his relationships with women, all lead to greater self-awareness. Questioning of his personal identity, reflections on his human condition, and above all considerations of the relationship between the male self and the female other, these are the harvest that Gille reaps from his journeying. At its most fundamental level Gille's "strange journey" is a journey into the discovery of self.

The central theme of the journey has, then, apart from its obvious and most literal sense, a threefold significance: it is a journey through decadent Western society; a journey through the experience of life toward a fuller understanding of the human condition; and finally, and most fundamentally, it is a journey into increased awareness of the self. These are the three closely related levels on which our examination of the novel will proceed.

Each stage of Gille's travels in France and Spain is marked at the outset by a clearly delineated image of social decadence. The first image evoked is that of the noble old country house in the Pyrenees that has suffered the ravages of the modern era's lack of taste and search for comfort. "The medieval period had established la Béraude as an impenetrable block between four towers, but middle-class patterns of living had taken it over and from century to century had settled comfortably into it" (9). Each century, from the seventeenth to the twentieth, has left its own particular mark on the structure, eating away at the medieval solidity by the removal of towers, the incorporation of windows, and the addition of pipes and wires necessary for modern comfort. Ugly nineteenth-century furniture completes the picture of an assault on the nobility and beauty of the past.

Through the image of "La Béraude" broad historical perspective is introduced into the novel and the portrayal of modern social decadence is set in a context that does not appear in earlier works. This is a context that will be further elaborated and given theoretical expression by Drieu in the essay *Notes pour comprendre le siècle* [Notes to Understand the Century, 1941], but its clearest expression in a work of fiction is to be found in this novel. "La Béraude" symbolizes Western society in the ages of its decline, and its final disintegration into the elements of nature is foreshadowed with a certain satisfaction: "Man thinks he is disturbing Nature, but his activity is simply one of its circuits; he can make no changes whatever to its order, which is also his own" (10). The harshness of a torrid summer further serves to emphasize the insignificance of man and his ephemeral creations and to reveal to one who is perceptive the precariousness of his human condition.

In such surroundings Gille spends his time with his friends and pays court in his bizarre fashion to Béatrix. The Cahen-Ducasse family, with the possible exception of Gabriel, forms a most unprepossessing group. They are wealthy and the young men are Jewish—for Drieu, the Jew is the most typical representative of modern bourgeois society; Yves is "a very feminine man" (14) and a homosexual; Baptiste has had experience of war but this has left him afflicted with a twitch that indicates a continuing fear of life (15); Gabriel has contracted a manifestly unsatisfactory marriage and neglects his wife for the English governess Rose Ramsay; and finally their stepmother has no children of her own, is sexually starved, and remains supremely respectful of social categories.

This family portrait of the modern bourgeoisie is complemented by a vision of the latter-day aristocracy in the form of Lord and Lady Owen and their naive daughter. Lord Owen is a comical caricature of a class which has allowed authority and power to slip from its grasp but which nevertheless excites the uncritical respect and envy of the bourgeoisie.

Sustained by a regular intake of whiskey, he appears as an almost speechless relic of a bygone era and moves without life or energy through the pages of the novel. Direction of his activities comes from a wife who rests secure in the knowledge that her title will continue after her husband's death. Little wonder that in such an environment Béatrix should confuse her social and financial attractiveness with the frank sensual appeal that Gille in his more idealistic moments prizes so greatly.

Gille meets Béatrix in the context of "La Béraude" but it is the Alhambra in Granada, described early in the second part of the novel, that provides the most appropriate image to present the decadence of the upper classes in modern times. The Alhambra is described as "the palace of the Arab aristocrats who died of refinement" (117), thus relating its former occupants to those who have progressively transformed "La Béraude" and now frequent it. The Arab princes have as their modern counterparts both the aristocrats who linger on lifelessly like Lord Owen and those who follow his daughter in her uncritical admiration of beauties they do not properly understand.

Gille's attraction to a *corrida* contrasts sharply with his refusal to play the tourist at the Alhambra. The simple enthusiasm of the crowd participating vicariously in this modern ritual of man's eternal fight for survival and search for food excites Gille's imagination. Here he finds a clear picture of the fundamentals of human existence, symbolized not only by the direct conflict between man and animal but also by the simple nobility of the arena's architecture, which recalls the form of the human body: "Moreover, this wall is a man's back; the structure is completely turned in toward the object of its delight like a man squatting in the sun" (119). The *corrida* also contrasts with the artificiality and refinement of the Alhambra—and by implication of "La Béraude" and its inhabitants—on the level of sexual relations. Gille is keenly aware of the sexual symbolism inherent in the "religious mystery" (122) that unfolds before him, and through it he becomes increasingly conscious of the socially induced poverty of sexual relations in his society.

In the early pages of the novel's third part Gille pays a brief visit to a Paris cinema, and it is this place of popular entertainment that serves as a third major, though briefly evoked, image to characterize modern aspirations and values and to set the tone for this part of the book. Once again it is the loss of contact with the realities of life that receives stress.

The cinema is characterized as a "big fantasy shop" and a "market for daydreams" (175), where the frustrations and contradictions of life may temporarily be resolved. In particular, the issues of love and money, relevant to Gille's situation, are mentioned: "All people desire love and money: outside, these two terms are contradictory; inside, through the facility of the dream, they come together. People come and wallow complacently in this illusory union" (176).

The decadence of "La Béraude," Granada, and Paris provides the framework for Gille's anxious efforts to understand the complexities and contradictions of his personality. These efforts are a constant feature of the various stages of his journeying through society and ultimately it is his quest for self-understanding and self-fulfillment that constitutes the novel's main theme. An indication of the importance of the theme is that the closing pages are almost totally given over to an analysis of Gille's personality by several of the characters including Gille himself.

The principal source of Gille's general dissatisfaction with his present state is his inability to break out of the restrictive confines of the self. Early in the novel, when out walking with Béatrix, he expresses the problem to himself in these terms: "[. . .] one must be very powerful to attain in a lasting way that solitude which never again becomes confused with egotism, which on the contrary becomes more and more open to the universal. Since the age of thirty his self had been starting to weigh on him with its annoying ways, its complacency, its habits. How could he break this self?" (79). The task Gille sets himself is to maintain an inner integrity, which he periodically associates with solitude, while at the same time opening himself to the profounder and broader aspects of life in a society which he sees as irremediably decadent.

Gille sees a relationship with woman as his best, and perhaps only, hope of achieving such a reconciliation between the self and the very principles of life. "The only remedy seemed to be to come into collision with this wretched little mystery of woman and to wound himself on it" (79). He proclaims woman as the "fetish" (313) of the unity he seeks, and with such religious and mystical notions in his mind he approaches Béatrix and later his mistress in Paris. Woman is for him a single principle, a mystical Earth Mother from whose unified substance various representations may be fashioned by man's hands. Woman is essentially malleable, but she nevertheless remains man's means of access to the "universal" (282–83).

With such an attitude it is scarcely surprising that the individual personalities of the women with whom Gille comes into contact receive scant recognition. For Gille every woman has a mask formed by social background, a mask which hides infinite possibilities of transformation. In Granada Gille holds the "beautiful mask" of Béatrix's face and muses: "It was a woman's mask, fine clay in which his fingers could mold whatever impression they desired and yet his fingers would forever remain impregnated with this particular substance after so many others" (282). When Gille is in Paris a letter from Béatrix evokes from him the conclusion that women are best considered as objects, as "fragments of the universe that take on life only beneath the gaze of man" (189).

Possibly the most startling evidence of Gille's tendency to depersonalize women is the fact that it is only on his return to Granada in December that he "sees" Béatrix for the first time—and finds her to his surprise to be ugly! Previously his vision of her has been expressed in the vaguest of terms. On their first meeting her features are barely mentioned, since "Gille liked to intoxicate himself, dewy-eyed, with a silhouette" (34). When Béatrix's personal attributes do receive Gille's closer attention, they are objectified and classified as befits the mask that they are. The extremes which this depersonalization process can reach are indicated by the fact that in a moment of rather grotesque fantasy he finds himself dreaming of "beautiful girls without heads, perhaps even without arms and without legs—trunks" (31). Such a vision is found desirable since it removes all trace of personality and in particular all "sentimental spice" (31).

This attitude to women—which falls so heavily on modern Western ears—shows Gille to be an irredeemable idealist and dreamer, a prey to many of the myths and fantasies that Western man has inherited, and unable to come to terms with the realities of his situation. At one moment he sees Béatrix as incorporating elements both of his dead mother and the Virgin Mary (145): she links in her person the female ideals of comforting earth mother and unsullied purity. At another moment Gille sees himself as the annunciatory angel, in purity bringing fecundity to the virgin and thus realizing the possibility of "love that is certain, which knows everything, which can do everything and which remains pure as gold, but which at the same time brings life to the very soul" (142). Small wonder that the women in Gille's life fail to measure up to his demands and that his initial enthusiasm should be replaced by disappointment and frustration!

One of the consequences of Gille's frustration in this and other areas is his attraction to violence, which is proclaimed not just as a principle of the natural order but also as a necessary element in human relations. It is also seen as needing to be exerted on the self to force it to emerge from its restrictive circle. Indeed, during the course of the novel Gille comes to recognize that violent action occupies a key place in his whole philosophy of life and that it is society's failure to recognize violence as a fundamental principle that is one of the roots of modern decadence.

We have already noted that the dominance of the natural world over man and his ephemeral works is proclaimed in the very first pages of the novel. Subsequently, attention is drawn to the pattern of unremitting violence which underlies what is euphemistically termed "the balance of nature." Gille's vision of the Pyrenees countryside, for example, is expressed in language strongly Darwinian in tone: "The peace, the deceptive peace, composed of millions of stifled acts of murder and destruction, the peace of the countryside howling out as unobtrusively as the peace of a city which, at night, chokes out behind shutters death rattles and entreaties" (60). Man, as part of this natural order, ignores such principles at his peril. Their validity, however, explains for Gille the continuing attraction of such rites as the *corrida* in a society in which man's elemental forces tend to be suppressed or neglected. Such thoughts also inform Gille's political attitudes, briefly mentioned in the course of the novel. His particular concern is for the fate of the "elemental forces" (157) of man beneath the discipline of a forcibly united Europe.

Man-woman relations are seen by Gille as lying within the context of this violent Darwinian view of life. On the first occasion that Béatrix goes walking with Gille she is shocked by the "fearful and delightful threat" of "this universal complicity of nature with love" (78), and it is significant that at this time it should be the violent aspects of the animal world that she notices: "Deep in the wood she could hear the cry of the beast of prey, the grievous cry of the beast enamored of its prey and, beneath the moon, weeping with desire" (78). Such expressions as "clever but rapidly executed tactic," "terrified," "favorable to the enemy" (78), "prey," "brutality," "desire to carry off" (34) are used when Béatrix and Gille come sexually close.

When visiting the Alhambra with Béatrix, Gille ponders what he terms his "eternal thought" (153): man needs to exercise his strength and for that reason constantly searches for something capable of providing the necessary resistance to him (153). For him in his present situation this resistance is Béatrix, "this scrap of clay in his two hands" (153). Shortly before, however, in conversation with Béatrix, he denies her claim that he despises women, adding the significant remark: "I do not scorn the clay of which my heart is made" (153). This remark elucidates the attitude of violence he has toward his own self: he finds within him the same femininity which in sexual relations calls for masterful, even violent, treatment. Consequently it is not surprising to find the same terminology of cruelty and violence used toward himself as toward the women he courts. For example, he speaks of his solitude, his unaccompanied and unchallenged self, in these terms: "His solitude was too facile; it had to be torn apart, it had to bleed" (79). Such words recur throughout the pages of the novel and justify Béatrix's claim that there is in her lover "the desire for self-abasement" (51). Even Johnny Hope recognizes the situation clearly enough to remark: "Try not to hurt others more than you hurt yourself" (158).

The reason for Gille's inner conflict, which leads him to take masochistic delight in failure that is often self-provoked, is that, despite his lofty ideals of mystical union with the universe, he sees himself as a willing victim of the decadence he condemns. He rails against the power of money and the soft decadence of modern life, but it is precisely to these "evils" that he is drawn. He condemns the modern cinemagoer for repairing to a world of dreams and losing contact with reality, yet he finds himself ready to indulge in "bourgeois" dreaminess to such an extent that one of his friends is led to say of him: "Yes, he's a fellow who is usually asleep, who makes a movement in life only when he is dreaming" (297). For such reasons he comes to doubt his personal identity (258) and to recognize in himself the hollowness and emptiness that he observes in others. The "strange journey" that Gille takes reveals him to be a personality at war within himself, unable to integrate and love himself and hence destined to wreak havoc in his efforts to love others. This psychological conflict informs his whole vision of reality, leads him to the attitudes toward nature of a Balzac or a Darwin, and condemns him to eternal flight. It is significant that, after pondering his reasons for leaving Béatrix and suggesting social decadence as the basic cause, Gille should finally abandon the attempt with the words: "Don't look for reasons" (318).

La Comédie de Charleroi

In bidding farewell to Béatrix at the end of *Drôle de voyage,* Gille says: "The time for love that is promising and hypocritical, tender and cruel is over. The time for the harsh equality of comradeship is at hand" (314). Within the context of the novel these words may be seen simply as an expression of Gille's disillusionment with love and women and a desperate turning to other areas of human involvement. In the light of Drieu's literature of the subsequent decade, however, the statement takes on much wider significance and indicates a change of emphasis: questions of social action and political commitment are to assume greater importance. *La Comédie de Charleroi* [The Comedy at Charleroi], a collection of six short war stories published in the year of Drieu's turning to fascism, 1934, is the first clear evidence in his fiction of this change.

The first and longest story bears the title of the whole collection and recounts a visit in 1919 to the battlefield of Charleroi in Belgium by the narrator and his employer, Madame Pragen. For this ostentatious, firmly bourgeois lady the visit is in the nature of a pilgrimage, since it was here that her son Claude, a member of the same regiment as the narrator, had fallen some five years before. Throughout the story contrasts are drawn between the reality of the battle as the narrator recalls it and the quite false idealized concepts that Madame Pragen chooses to cherish: "She had wanted, abstractly as it were, to see the spot where her son had died; but not the spot where he had been killed. She didn't know what war was and she didn't want to know" (57). Her basic motivation in coming to Charleroi is to parade her wealth and stress her social prestige to the local inhabitants. They in their turn at least appear to take seriously her role as the worthy parent of a military "hero" in the hope that they may benefit from her anticipated largesse. Such sordid social exchange tends to fade, however, before the living memories that are provoked in the narrator by the reality of the battlefield before him. On the one hand he is reminded of the dehumanizing aspects of modern warfare: "In former days, war was men on their feet. War today is all the postures of shame" (31). On the other hand he cannot forget the extraordinary exultation he experienced in leading a charge, abortive though it proved to be, against the enemy. This was for him nothing less than a mystical experience, and in a highly lyrical outburst he exclaims: "Suddenly, I knew myself, I knew my life. So that was my life, that impulse which was never again to cease" (70). Such moments, however, are shortlived, and the descent to the mundane realities of despised modern life follows as inevitably as the return to Paris with Madame Pragen.

"Le Chien de l'écriture" [The Charm of the Written Word] also has as one of its principal themes the contrast between the reality of a wartime situation and the falsification of this reality after the war has ended. Grummer, a cavalry sergeant, is attached to the narrator's infantry division stationed in the forests of Lorraine. When the division is moved to Verdun to take part in the battle that is to cost so many lives, he uses his wealthy and influential connections behind the lines to have himself transferred to a less dangerous area. After the war the narrator encounters Grummer by chance in a cinema and hears him boasting to his lady friend of the part he had played in the battle of Verdun, which is being presented with only partial accuracy on the screen. The story closes with a silent confrontation between Grummer and the narrator, who is left wondering whether Grummer is at heart an irredeemable coward or whether he was simply a more obvious victim of the fear that afflicted every soldier.

The only story of the collection to have a wartime setting outside France is "Le Voyage des Dardanelles" [The Journey to the Dardanelles], which recounts the narrator's experiences and reflections as he travels with a group of volunteers from Normandy to Marseille, thence to the Dardanelles. Although the latter part of the story tells of an indecisive encounter with the Turks, the dominant emphasis is upon relationships between the narrator and his fellow volunteers and also upon his own fears and the conflicts of his personality within the context of the stresses of war.

This reflective, psychological emphasis is continued in "Le Lieutenant de tirailleurs" [The Tirailleur Lieutenant] and "Le Déserteur" [The Deserter]. In the former, the contrast in the first two stories of the collection between reality and its idealization acquires a further dimension. In a Marseille bar in 1917 the narrator discusses the nature of war with a professional soldier, a lieutenant from a Moroccan infantry regiment. The conversation centers on the degradation of modern mechanized "democratic" warfare, which is contrasted with the more "human" battles of the Middle Ages when courage was allowed adequate expression. One particular reaction to the horrors of contemporary war is treated in "Le Déserteur." Some eleven years after the end of World War I the narrator, on a government economic mission to South America, is induced to speak to a man who deserted from the

French army in August 1914. His decision to flee from the consequences of narrow nationalism in Europe is one which the narrator finds difficult to challenge since he, too, even now, is tempted to opt out of a society whose values he cannot accept. The title of the story consequently refers not just to the deserter's flight at the outset of war but also to the temptation of a far profounder desertion from contemporary society by both speakers.

The final story of the collection, "La Fin d'une guerre" [The End of a War], returns to the war years when the narrator is attached to the American forces as an interpreter. Even in this position the same problems of reality and dream, commitment and flight pursue him. On what he himself terms an "absurd impulse" (298) he asks an American general, whose bravery he greatly admires, to allow him to accompany him to the front line on the following day. The American general acknowledges the urge for self-testing that provokes such a request but puts the visit off until the day after. In the meantime the narrator happens to see the horribly disfigured face of an officer being carried back from the area that he himself had asked to visit. Such a sight causes him to reflect upon the futility of his animal urge to display courage, and this leads him to show greater restraint in the future.

All six stories may be seen as having a common point of reference in the charge at Charleroi. This incident, to which Drieu refers in numerous other writings as the focal point of his life, comes in the first months of the war, and all the narrator's subsequent experience, whether in France or abroad, at the front or behind the lines, tends to be viewed in relation to this moment of mystical exaltation. But, as Proust reminds us, such moments are rare—perhaps even unique—and it is the narrator's progressive awareness of this fact that produces the nostalgia for the remote past and the disillusionment with the present that inform the whole collection. Each story refers, directly or indirectly, to Charleroi as an expression of man's basic need to try his strength against that of his fellows, but modern technological warfare renders such acts of heroic initiative futile and anachronistic. It is in this sense that modern war is regarded as fundamentally inhuman: not so much because of its cruelty and horror, but rather because it crushes the "fighting instinct" which had received such fleeting expression early in the war. By preventing man from "giving meaning to his courage" (255), modern war provides yet another illustration for Drieu of the decadence of contemporary life.

One of the key elements of Drieu's castigation of modern war is that it isolates the individual and condemns him to inactivity. In the first story the narrator speaks of "the abominable solitude of the modern battlefield" (53) with each man crouching terrified and passive in his trench as the shells and bullets whistle overhead. Group action is discouraged since it attracts concentrated enemy fire and hence increases the probability of death. It is, however, precisely comradeship and communion that men need at such moments, as Grummer discovers when danger threatens: "He was no longer the same man. He looked at us suddenly with other eyes. He was going to confront death, he needed companions" (142). The moment of the charge at Charleroi represents, among other things, an assertion of this need of comradeship and it is significant that this should be expressed through action. For a fleeting moment the realities of the situation are forgotten and the "most heroically passive cattle" (33) are united by action in an instinctive protest against the "postures of shame" that they have been obliged to adopt. Virile communal action emerges as a necessary expression of man's humanity, but in modern times it has become suicidal folly.

In Drieu's portrayal of wartime conditions there is ample illustration of another aspect of his vision of modern decadence: the decline of effective leadership. Every stage of the battle at Charleroi, for example, is closely associated with questions of leadership. The narrator's first act of initiative comes as a response to the inability of one of his officers to take decisive action. He forces this officer to give him a dangerous assignment as a runner, and this incident impresses upon him the vital role of effective leadership at all levels of society: "I was penetrating to the essence of war, to the essence of society, the question of leadership" (41). In modern warfare, however, those in command, the generals and the politicians, "the old half-witted hierarchy" (69), have no contact with the realities of the action, while officers of lower rank on the battlefield inspire only scorn.

The experience of the charge itself is intimately related to the question of leadership. Initially the need is felt for someone to express the general will to action of the men by emerging from cover and leading the attack: the decisive act of a leader is required. Moreover, once the act is performed, the transformation that takes place in the narrator is also seen essentially in terms of leadership. A "new being" emerges, one that is felt to have greater personal authenticity in that it reveals hitherto suppressed qualities: "I had felt palpitating within me a prisoner ready to burst forth. A prisoner of the life that had been made for me, that I had made for myself. A prisoner of the crowd, of sleep, of humility" (70). The "prisoner" is identified as a leader, but it is noteworthy that this new "leader" is seen not in strictly personalized terms but rather as the fullest expression of what is truly human in man: "A leader is a man at his peak; one who gives and takes in the same ejaculation" (70). The leadership experience of the charge does not bring separation and isolation from others but involvement and identification with their true humanity.

It is precisely at this point that the reason for the extraordinary importance assumed by the charge at Charleroi becomes apparent. Only then are the problems and contradictions of the "self" resolved. During the charge the "self" is fully expressed, but inherent in such expression is the capacity to transcend the narrow confines of the narrator's individuality to absorb and merge with those around him in a new elite united by action: "I wanted to take possession of all these men around me, to increase myself with them, to increase them through me and to project all of us together with me at the head, across the universe" (70). For once the dimly glimpsed but constantly affirmed unity of life is realized. "At that moment I felt the unity of life. The same gesture to eat and to love, to act and to think, to live and to die. Life is one single movement forward" (73). For one so obsessed with the problems of the self as Drieu, the charge at Charleroi remains a demanding standard by which to judge later experience.

The revelation of the profundity of the self at Charleroi does in fact haunt the pages of the succeeding stories. Perhaps its clearest expression is in "Le Voyage des Dardanelles" where a desperate plea for intensity of living is related to being alone and unknown, but at the same time "lost and immersed in the throng of peoples" (188). All social ties are renounced, whether they involve family, friends, or finance, present responsibilities or future prospects. In this way he will be socially "naked"—a word which recurs in this context—and hence free to express with and through others the fundamental features of manhood. He will become "a man who has restored in himself the rudiments of all reality, who works with his hands and his feet, who eats, who drinks, who sleeps" (189).

The nature of the self is also one of the principal themes of "Le Chien de l'écriture," but here the aspect of the self that is revealed is of a rather different nature from that of the Charleroi memory. The story treats not just the cowardice of one man, Grummer, but also, and perhaps more fundamentally, the question of fear, that basic visceral fear, that "huge female" (152) that men in battle discover to be part of their very being. Certain parts of the film of Verdun remind the narrator of an occasion when, under bombardment, his fear had been at its most extreme, and the groan that he involuntarily utters now in the cinema recalls the terror of the cry that had at that time issued from the "depths of [his] soul" (155). In this cry the narrator claims to have learned more about himself than in the rest of his experience of life, and the present "echo of that tragic power" (156) proclaims the continuing presence of the wartime lesson.

"Le Chien de l'écriture" and "La Comédie de Charleroi" are thus complementary in the sense that they illustrate differing aspects of the same self as it is revealed under the stresses of war. Fear and the impulse to courage are seen as twin elements of the human personality, both of them capable of independent expression and neither able to be eliminated. The narrator's ideal appears to be in fact a productive interaction of the two. During the description of the charge he proclaims: "It is not a matter of overcoming fear with courage but of dissolving fear in courage and courage in fear and of springing forward at the extreme tip of the experience" (71). Only in this way can the full intensity of life be experienced. Indeed such interaction of courage and fear, and in particular the continuing effort to prevent fear from gaining the upper hand, informs to a large degree all six stories of the collection.

But, in the context of the modern age, of what possible relevance are questions of individual courage and fear when the creations of man's technology and the social attitudes they express mock the efforts of those who would assert their humanity? This question is specifically posed in "Le Lieutenant de tirailleurs" and "Le Déserteur" as—apart from a brief interlude—the sphere of action moves from the immediate theater of war to a broader discussion of the options that present themselves to man in the twentieth century.

In these stories the narrator engages in conversation with men who, in their separate ways, have chosen to desert European society and its conflicts. The professional soldier, having been confirmed in his hatred of the modern world by his experience of the front, has chosen to return to Morocco where he believes he will find a situation more in conformity with his idealized Middle Ages. He is pictured as a latter-day Noah, fleeing the "European flood" for the safety of his "ark" across the Mediterranean. The deserter who gives his name to the fifth story has likewise fled across the seas, but for reasons which are apparently less noble. Preeminent for him is personal preservation and he does not seek to rationalize his fear and egocentrism.

In the conversation between these two "deserters" and the narrator we have an interesting projection of the debate raging within the narrator's own mind as he seeks to decide how he should react to the decadence of his own society. The choice is clear: acceptance and commitment or refusal and desertion. The underlying issues are, however, considerably more complex and far less certain. How can he be sure that the lieutenant's decision (and his own temptation) to opt out is genuinely inspired by disgust with the modern world and does not spring from fear as craven as that of the South American deserter? May it not be that the lieutenant, despite his assertions, is simply "a modern, delicate man, one who has not been prepared from childhood for misery, for the terrible destiny of man" (245)? Moreover, what credence can be placed in the romantic picture of medieval society that he shares with this man? Is this not simply a sophisticated means of escaping the commitment to one's age that is sensed as a duty?

In both "Le Lieutenant de tirailleurs" and "Le Déserteur" it is the narrator who, frequently without obvious conviction, pleads the case for commitment as the only course for one anxious to fulfill his role as a man. His attitude is best summed up in his words: "I am quite aware that I would cease being human and would withdraw all reality from the rest of my days if I completely cut myself off from that crowd and its wretchedness" (244). He has, however, few convincing arguments to offer for the course he commends and he finds himself in basic agreement with the analysis of society made by his two interlocutors. His choice to work in a decadent society does not claim to be rationally motivated; it is rather a desperate, essentially instinctive attempt to overcome what may be construed as weakness and to preserve at least the possibility of the "true humanity" glimpsed during the charge. The mirage of Charleroi will continue to be pursued.

The narrator's choice of social involvement rather than individualistic retreat makes his request to the American general in "La Fin d'une guerre" more than an act of bravado. What he terms an attack of his "old sickness" (299), a thirst for action, had made him, despite his wounds, volunteer for active service in 1917. "That self that is in me and that appreciates simple devotion, rectitude, unqualified courage, commitment to a cause" (307) now elicits the request needlessly to face the dangers of the front line. Refusal to allow expression to this superior self deprives life of all value: "Running from death is dying" (309). As in the two preceding stories, involvement is chosen not for pragmatic reasons, but rather to induce the individual self to experience the intensity of life. Hence the exercise is one of self-testing, self-conquest, and self-control. "For me it was a question of knowing once more whether I had faith or not" (311). In typical Drieu fashion, the story, and with it the collection, closes on an indecisive and enigmatic note that borders on psychological defeat. The sight of the horribly wounded man causes the other "cynical, cunning" (308) self that constantly advocates withdrawal and isolation to reassert itself. The final pages are full of the horrors of war, and the narrator, numbed by what he has witnessed, expresses not reluctance but relief when the announcement is made that his division is to retire from the front line.

In an article published in 1929, Drieu referred to the war poems of *Interrogation* as "a somewhat suspect writing"[2] and added that he was anxious to compose another work that would correct certain of the impressions that had been conveyed by his first literary venture. In particular he wished to refute those who had seen in him an unqualified apologist of war. This is the most obvious reason for Drieu's turning back to the war years in *La Comédie de Charleroi,* but, as our analysis has shown, the work goes much deeper than this. It is true that the horror and especially the inhumanity of modern warfare receive considerable stress, but the whole experience is set firmly in the context of the decadence of an entire society, within which the individual seeks his definition and his role.

The search for the self in *La Comédie de Charleroi* differs from that of earlier works principally in its sense of urgency. There is a pressing conviction that the time has come for the resolution of basic issues, and to find his answers Drieu abandons the decadent triviality of peacetime for the elemental "nudity" of the battlefield. As "La Comédie de Charleroi" and "Le Chien de l'écriture" vividly show, Drieu believes that man's moral extremes of exultant courage and cringing terror become manifest under fire and that the full intensity of living lies in their creative fusion.

The reason for the urgency appears in the second half of the collection, especially in "Le Lieutenant de tirailleurs" and "Le Déserteur," where the degree and direction of one's social involvement are seen as questions that demand immediate answers. The earlier initial tension between fear and courage is transposed into a pressing, inescapable choice between serving society and rejecting it. The choice is set, of course, against the background of the late war years, but it seems clear that in this largely autobiographical work Drieu is using such a background to express current concerns. For Drieu the early 1930s marked the end of an age, so that the involvement of the individual in establishing creative new directions for society was a question of considerable importance.

The stories make it equally clear, however, that social organization is considered important not for its tangible achievements but for its capacity to allow the self to experience life at its most intense. The narrator judges peacetime by the values that had emerged at Charleroi. He suggests this in a moment of wistful regret in "Le Lieutenant de tirailleurs" when he refers to "that kind of revolutionary, initially a warrior, that I vainly sought after the war in the French parties" (247). His commitment is not to a social program but to a largely undefined ideal of individual initiative and corporate action, which at times degenerates into a distasteful Nietzschean worship of strength and violence for their own sake.

La Comédie de Charleroi is Drieu's best-known collection of short stories and reveals him as a master of the genre. His talents are perhaps most obvious in the first story, which, as we have seen, in some essential respects sets the tone for the rest of the collection. The portrayal of Madame Pragen in the opening pages is highly evocative and the manner in which her bourgeois bombast gradually fades before the remembered realities of the battle is one of Drieu's outstanding pieces of writing. The abstract terms in which she delights then give way to a vocabulary of concrete objects whose reality is almost palpable. "Each man was scraping away with his shovel in front of him. There were meadows and fields of stubble. In the meadows, cows abandoned by the Belgian peasants and in the fields the recently cut wheat, still there, in sheaves" (23–24). The poetic prose of the charge, moreover, conveys the exultation of the moment in terms that recapture the youthful enthusiasm of *Interrogation*.

Apart from the constant echo of the charge at Charleroi and the common background of war, each story deals in its particular fashion with questions of desertion and commitment, fear and courage, and each involves some degree of personal failure. But within the context of these common features a clear line of development emerges. In general terms this development takes the reader through the war years. A less obvious but ultimately more significant development, however, is that which leads from the attempt to probe and define the self in the first three stories to the inquiry into personal response to social organization that, broadly speaking, characterizes the latter three. In consequence *La Comédie de Charleroi* emerges as a delicately structured whole, each of whose parts is nevertheless capable of standing alone.

Drieu himself considered *La Comédie de Charleroi* as one of his best and most important works, on one occasion referring to it as his first "work of human dimensions."[3] Written at a time of obvious personal crisis, it is one of the profoundest, most honest investigations of the self. What made the work so dear to Drieu's heart was presumably that it centered on the "eternity of that minute" (77) which he had experienced at Charleroi. From a literary point of view, however, the importance issues principally from the fact that this investigation of the self is conducted through the agency of people taking part in events that are vibrant with reality. The self is sought not through tranquil reflection or through the frustration of life in a decadent society but in the context of action in a climate of harsh necessity. The path to the future is, rather ironically for Drieu, sought through resurrection of the past.

Journal d'un homme trompé

The year 1934 saw the publication by Drieu of another collection of short stories or episodes under the title *Journal d'un homme trompé* [Diary of a Man Betrayed]. With the exception of "Défense de sortir" [Departure Forbidden] (which in his collected *Ecrits de jeunesse* of 1941 Drieu included with the writings of *Le jeune Européen*), the stories treat a wide variety of man-woman relationships in contemporary society. Frank confessions stand alongside satirical portraits of marriage in the bourgeoisie, and the ravages of jealousy are contrasted with those rare occasions when a man and a woman form a united couple. Inevitably one finds some restatement of situations encountered in earlier novels and short stories, but the collection remains distinctive and important through the comprehensive way it treats the fragility of links between the sexes. In it one finds Drieu's most clearly expressed statement of belief about the nature of woman's expectations in love, together with an analysis of her reactions when these expectations are disappointed.

As a background to this analysis there is also a bitter condemnation of male weakness mediated through a particular interpretation of the figure of Don Juan.

It may appear strange that Drieu should have published such a work in the same year as the war reminiscences of *La Comédie de Charleroi* and the political essay *Socialisme fasciste* [Fascist Socialism]. Common to all three, however, is a search for intensity through conscious involvement. As the mystical ideal of union with others through personal commitment to intense action haunts the pages of the war stories following the experience of Charleroi, so a dimly glimpsed ideal of love through an enduring relationship between a man and a woman informs the catalog of sexual misery and disharmony of *Journal d'un homme trompé*. In love as in war commitment that is both self-effacing and self-fulfilling is sought, and this also determines the political philosophy expressed in *Socialisme fasciste*.

The only enduring relationship in *Journal d'un homme trompé* to come close to Drieu's ideal of intensity is treated in "Le bon moment" [The Right Moment]. The story is in three sections, each presenting a different approach to the ten years of married life of the couple Marc and Gisèle. The first section deals with the attitude of Marc, who is facing death after an air accident in Tchad; the second section reveals the thoughts of Gisèle, who remains unaware of her husband's plight; while the final section introduces, in the person of Bernard Boulanger, the social attitudes that have been a continual threat to the happiness of the couple.

The fidelity of Marc and Gisèle to each other comes from an attitude of total personal commitment, particularly on the part of Gisèle. Boulanger remarks that Gisèle "was born and will die in the world of the wager, the world of the single love, the world of marriage" (156), and he is aware that the richness of the ten years during which this "wager" has lasted has left an indelible impression upon her. Speculating upon the death of Marc in Africa, Boulanger describes the woman he would like to make his mistress as "a nun who has been cast out of her convent and who cannot now adapt to the movements of the century" (158). The price to be paid for such intense personal commitment is inadaptability to current social values and the consequent inability to form another comparable relationship. Mathilde, a friend, attributes Gisèle's fidelity to pride or lethargy, and Gisèle acknowledges the partial truth of such a statement. Her years with Marc have left her emotionally exhausted: "One cannot love twice, it is too tiring" (155).

The title of the story refers to the death of Marc, which is "timely" in the sense that both parties are aware that the intensity of their union is beginning to wane. On the one hand Marc begins to regret the demands and sacrifices he has imposed on his wife, unaware that it is precisely the intensity of her self-giving that has brought such happiness to the marriage. On the other hand Gisèle, despite herself, finds that she is increasingly vulnerable to the poisonous suggestions of her friends and is even beginning to doubt the reality of her full personal involvement in the ten-year experience. Her diary closes with these words addressed to Marc: "Ah, I would like you never to return, since I am mourning the death of both of us" (155). True to the myth world of romantic love so dear to Drieu, death accedes to this instinctively formulated request by striking down Marc and preserving from the deterioration of time "something indestructible, a fixed radiating force that ravages the past and the future, one of the forces of fatality" (158).

Most of the female protagonists of *Journal d'un homme trompé* share Gisèle's attitude of selfless devotion, but none expresses it more clearly or with greater intensity than Rosita, the girl whose story Gille recounts in "Rien n'y fait" [All of no Avail]. Gille meets Rosita in Morocco, far from the distractions of Paris. After two happy months together Rosita announces to Gille that she has broken with the man who has supported her for five years and who is at present preparing to provide for her future. Scorning financial security, she proclaims her readiness to return to Paris with Gille and to face with him the uncertainties of his way of life. Back in the environment of Paris all Gille's weaknesses emerge, especially his jealousy, which shows itself in a demand that his mistress reveal the facts of her past life. In all she has encountered four men: she suffered betrayal at the hands of a rich young property owner with whom she went to live at the age of twenty; she was treated with brutality by Antonio, a professional dancer; then she had resorted to prostitution before coming under the protection of the man she abandons to follow Gille. The forced revelation of these sordid aspects of her past does not fail to poison the present relationship. Gille's jealousy feeds on these details that Rosita had been trying to forget and he begins to neglect her. One day she leaves him to return to Morocco, where she dies of a sudden illness three months later.

In this confession by Gille of the moral destruction wrought by his jealousy, it is Rosita's purity and integrity and above all her utter self-giving that emerge most clearly. Even after the suffering she has undergone from men who have proved unworthy of her fidelity, she retains "a rather proud idea of men" (81) which is sufficiently strong for her to sacrifice security and follow Gille into uncertainty. In so doing she becomes, in the author's eyes, an exemplary figure who seeks self-fulfillment in love through self-giving.

The selflessness that is presented by Drieu in such stories as "Rien n'y fait" as a desirable, because a fundamental, part of the female personality may, of course, be regarded as an expression of his reactionary antifeminism—an attitude which these days would provoke the charge of male chauvinism. Such a view doubtless has its validity but it is only fair to note that for Drieu loss of individuality is posited as a condition of self-fulfillment in love, whether the individual be male or female. In this way such figures as Rosita become exemplary not only as an expression of desired female attitudes but also as an expression of the relationship of love itself. In the first and longest story, which bears the name of the collection as a whole and which has Gille as narrator, such a view of love is stated on numerous occasions. In speaking of himself and his mistress Nelly, Gille idealizes their relationship and refers to it as "the coincidence of two acts of giving," "the dissolution of two beings into one," and as "the absence of egoism but the fulfillment of being" (30). It is therefore not surprising that the vocabulary of mysticism, with its loss of the sense of self, should at times intrude into descriptions of sexual relationships. Gille justifies such an intrusion with the parenthesis: "[. . .] if a mystical writing always seems to be a transposed description of the sexual act, a sexual analysis in its turn attracts mystical vocabulary" (30).

In the description of actual love relationships as they are portrayed in this collection of stories, mystical vocabulary is rarely warranted, however. For this situation Drieu holds men to be totally responsible, and it is this view of male inadequacy that produces his particular interpretation of Don Juan. The figure of Don Juan emerges in the very first pages of "Journal d'un homme trompé," where he is presented as a "coward" (15). He skips from woman to woman not because he is in search of some unattainable ideal or because he has exhausted the possibilities of each woman, but rather because of his fear of having his inadequacies revealed and of being replaced by another lover. Such an interpretation of this fascinating figure of one of the basic Western myths of love is further developed in "Les Caprices de la jalousie" [The Caprices of Jealousy]. Here, in response to his friend's view of Don Juan as a rapid accumulator of profound conquests, Gille states: "It is my deep conviction that one is loved to the precise extent that one loves. Now, since Don Juan did not take time to love, he did not give women time to love him" (189). Gille refuses to apply the term love to the first necessarily shallow emotion which is as far as Don Juan can ever reach in his amorous pursuits.

Although Don Juan is mentioned by name in only two of the stories of the collection, the weakness that characterizes him is reflected in the actions of almost all the male characters portrayed. In "Journal d'un homme trompé" Gille is in full flight from a mistress who is suspected of infidelity. Flight is first experienced as freedom from the servitudes of women and society, but awareness soon comes that it is simply a manifestation of weakness, a refusal to come to terms with a challenging situation. In the ironically titled "Un bon ménage" [A Happy Household], Violette, the wife of a successful architect, René Dalley, despairs of her husband's weakness and takes a lover, only to relive the experience of Flaubert's Emma Bovary, who found in adultery "all the platitudes of marriage." "Haunted by weak men" (58), Violette finds greater emotional intensity in the bitterness of her weeping than in the company of those who merely desire her body.

The male weakness that brings unhappiness to Violette Dalley and to many of the other women characters of *Journal d'un homme trompé* is linked on several occasions with what is seen as a modern attempt to separate the "soul" from the "body." This phenomenon is extensively explored in *Notes pour comprendre le siècle* some six years later, when it is seen as one of the basic factors leading to the social and political decadence of modern times. Already here, however, its pernicious effects on the unity of the self and hence on the capacity to love are given ample illustration. In the analysis she makes of her situation, Violette Dalley is rather more clear-sighted than her sisters in distress when she says of herself: "Her soul would remain here and her body would go elsewhere. She clearly glimpsed the infinite possibilities that were being lost, the profound misery that would ensue for this soul and for this body that the power of a man could have blended into a single big growing being, interweaving the rich possibilities of spirit and body, multiplying itself in constant images, in a palace rich in mirrors" (57).

Love is a fusion of two individual selves, which may reflect, heighten, and develop the richness of human personality, but only insofar as these selves resist and overcome the tendencies toward division and fragmentation.

The responsibility of the male for affirming in himself and promoting in women the unity of soul and body emerges as an underlying principle in the short stories and is recognized by the more perceptive characters. Gille, for example, when speaking of his mistress, confesses his shortcomings in these terms: "My love could have made her focus her energies on herself and made her burst forth in total giving. And the constant exercise of such total giving would have gradually endowed her with strong unity" (33). Later in the book, in the context of his definition of Don Juan, Gille distinguishes between "intellectual knowledge" and the deeper self-involving experience of "amorous knowledge" (189). He condemns Don Juan, whose attitudes he himself nevertheless mirrors, for limiting himself to the former. For Drieu, "intellectual" tends to connote "superficial" and in this example it reflects—perhaps a little strangely—the further distinction that he makes in human sexual relations between "pleasure" and "love." The use of the intellect and the experience of pleasure are necessary preliminaries to the penetration of life's mysteries, but they prove inadequate to one who relies on them alone. "In a brothel, men and women cultivate virginity of the heart" (22).

These examples show that the weakness of which Gille is so painfully conscious in himself and which causes the women characters of *Journal d'un homme trompé* such emotional distress is presented by Drieu as a basic inability to conceive and assert the wholeness of the self. Don Juan and his ilk prove inadequate in matters of love because they are truncated and incomplete as persons. They are unable or unwilling to recognize the unity and the richness of their own selves and hence deny such a discovery to the women they court. The jealousy that destroys so many of the relationships in the short stories and which presents itself as a lack of self-confidence is simply one widespread example of this basic shortcoming.

The women that Drieu studies in the pages of this book express in various ways their frustration at being deprived of the possibility of self-realization. Two of the female reactions treated are the assumption of a compensatory masculinity and the transference of their affections to something nonhuman.

In her initial attempts to preserve her threatened marriage, Violette Dalley assumes the traditional male role of protector and sustainer. She attempts to construct about her husband a barrier against the temptations of the surrounding world and succeeds in making him feel "judged, evaluated, hemmed in, dominated" (50). This intrusion into the realm of male responsibility has disastrous consequences not only for the marriage, which is further weakened, but also for Violette's own personality. The openness that had previously attracted men is no longer there, and they tend to be repelled and even intimidated by the harshness which has replaced it: "[. . .] if people noticed that she did retain something of herself, it clearly appeared to be just for herself, she was a woman who had become closed" (54). "Divorcées" [Divorced Women] likewise analyses the hardening of a woman's personality and also treats her complex relations with the friend she believes to have alienated her husband's affections.

The transference of a woman's affections to something nonhuman is studied in "La Femme au chien" [The Woman with the Dog]. In a hotel at Cannes, which with its region is painted in the somber colors of decadence at the outset of the story, Gille hears the woman in the next room indulging in a monologue of child's talk, which he finally discovers is directed at her dog. It is clear to him that the dog has taken the place of a lover or a child. What chiefly distresses him is that with this animal none of the fundamental problems of life arise, since it has been conformed totally to the lifeless world of the woman who remains alone: "The lady wanted only one thing: to distort the animal nature of Bijou and, with life's complications removed, to play at being people with him. A son or a mute lover, more convenient, more manageable, less tiring" (95). In this story all Drieu's antifeminist reactionary views are expressed, and this woman's world without a male is seen as a prison, the four walls of which guard her from genuine contact with life. The image is, however, pursued further. Recognizing the resemblances between his own isolation and that of the woman, Gille remarks: "And these four walls are the walls of the self, from which we scarcely ever emerge, to which we constantly return" (92).

A related but somewhat different question of human psychology is raised in "La Voix" [The Voice]. Gille is in Rome, and, as he ponders the grandeur of a civilization now dead, his reflections are interrupted by memories of his own past: he recognizes the voice of Valentine, the woman who had once been his wife. What strikes him above all about her voice is the decline in its tone and quality, a symptom of what he senses as a fundamental change in her personality: "That voice, once palpitating with life, was like a dead fish in a net, it was no longer vibrant. It had become impervious and no longer drew sustenance from the quivering life of the universe" (68). Moreover, there is now no trace in her voice and in the personality it expresses of his own influence which had been so strong in former years.

This chance encounter and the observations it provokes lead Gille to reflect upon the connections between human relationships, memory, and personality. How is it possible that he, who had once been part of Valentine's very substance, could be apparently so completely forgotten? Does the change in Valentine's voice indicate the suppression of an ineradicable part of her personality? Is human memory ever able to suppress moments of intensity? Or is it like the processes of nature, destructive of what no longer has life and directed to the intensity of the present? "Is then Humanity only Nature? Is not memory stronger than the earth? Do we rot away in the hearts of those who have loved us as we do in the humus of the grave?" (70). Gille chooses to comfort himself with a theory of the ultimate preservation in an unknown "heaven" of the intense moments of human experience, but finally the questions he asks remain without conclusive answers. They do, however, serve to give a philosophical dimension to the work's investigation of man-woman relationships by relating them to the ideas on the growth and decline of societies treated in other works.

Journal d'un homme trompé is Drieu's most obvious attempt to present as objective a picture as he is able of man-woman relationships in his society. The eleven stories of the collection not only contain a wide variety of characters and situations but display a considerable effort to present as many different points of view as possible. The Gille of *L'Homme couvert de femmes* and *Drôle de voyage* remains the main character of two stories and a major participant in one other. However, while he himself is the diarist in "Journal d'un homme trompé" and recounts personally the story of his jealousy in "Rien n'y fait", the encounter of "La Voix" is related by two of his friends. In each of the other stories the narrator remains anonymous, and this not only leaves the author a certain freedom of expression, but helps to create the impression of an interested but relatively objective observer. It is clear that in this approach to the short story Drieu is experimenting with ways of resolving his continuing problem of how an involved individual can present a valid picture of his society.

Drieu's experimentation is also evident in the literary form given to the stories. "Journal d'un homme trompé" is composed of a succession of diary entries, at first very brief but lengthening with the growing complexity of the relationship treated; "Le bon moment" mingles diary entries with reported conversation; "Défense de sortir" is in the nature of a philosophical tale; "Rien n'y fait" is a confessional narrative; while the remaining stories mingle conversation with third-person narration. Such variety of form and technique helps to increase the interest of the situation described and serves to illustrate the attention given to literary technique by a writer who would have us believe that his writing is as inconsistent and imperfect as the life he led.

Beloukia

Beloukia (1936) was Drieu's first "exotic" novel in the sense that it has its setting in ancient Baghdad with all the color that that name evokes and has characters who are non-European. The story relates the course of the secret liaison between the princess Beloukia and the poet Hassib. Hassib is a follower of Abdul, an enemy of the caliph and currently engaged in plotting his overthrow, while Beloukia's husband, Mansour, is the caliph's chief adviser. Since the fall of the caliph would almost certainly topple Mansour and perhaps bring disgrace and even death to Beloukia and her children, Hassib finds himself torn between his ideologically based political allegiance and his passion for the princess. This classical struggle between loyalty to a cause and love of a woman constitutes the novel's fundamental framework into which the various elements of the work are set.

In his analysis of *Beloukia,* Frédéric Grover remarks on the frequent use of the verb *déchirer* ("to rend"),[4] and it is indeed true that concepts of tension and painful rupture, with the contrasting ideas of harmony and unification that they presuppose, tend to dominate the patterns of thought that Drieu expresses through his characters. The relationship between Hassib and Beloukia, continually threatened by the presence of the husband, is described on one occasion as "delightful and rent asunder" (60) and this alternation, with the tension it brings, characterizes not only all the interpersonal relationships that are treated in the novel but also the individual personality of almost every character. The happiness of Hassib and Beloukia is, for example, threatened from within as well as from without: by the internal contradictions of Hassib as well as by the externally imposed constraints that prevent them from being together. Such circumstances create a situation of intense psychological conflict which brings to the novel a complexity that its exotic facade may initially tend to hide.

At the time of the events described in the novel, Hassib has been Beloukia's lover for a period of three years. During this time the relationship has brought blissful happiness to both, fulfilling the promise of their first meeting. Moreover, the danger which Beloukia runs in paying regular visits to her lover's house and in being with him even when she is travelling in foreign parts serves to heighten the intensity of their relationship by focusing all attention on the external threats that are constantly present. At several points in the story it is even suggested that physical danger is a guarantee of their love in that it prevents more subtle threats to their liaison from emerging.

The necessity for Hassib to choose between love and political allegiance produces in him a painful psychological awakening. Up to this moment the joys of the relationship have been sufficient to obscure for him many aspects of the humiliating "sharing" of Beloukia with Mansour. In particular, he has succeeded in suppressing the question of the role he plays in the totality of his mistress's life. Is he the dominant element in her life, or is he simply one part in a rich existence which includes a powerful husband, cherished children, wealth, comfort, and security? Such questions now begin to press upon his consciousness, and with them come a flood of others which swamp the blind trust that has hitherto bound the couple together. Hassib is forced to recognize his need to occupy a situation of unchallenged dominance in Beloukia's life, but he becomes less and less convinced that this need is being met. As doubt feeds upon doubt, he grows progressively more jealous of all the aspects of Beloukia's life from which he is excluded.

This crisis of doubt and jealousy, whose genesis, development, and attempted resolution constitute the main thread of the novel, reaches its peak in the central and longest chapter. By a subterfuge Hassib makes his way into Mansour's house with the professed purpose of warning Beloukia of the threat to the life of Hassan, her son. Once inside, however, his thoughts and actions make him aware that his real motivation is otherwise: "But this pressing necessity now seemed to him to be merely a pretext to feel the terrible excitement of suddenly being at the heart of the mystery of his life. This desire to be on the other side of Beloukia's life, that was what he had suppressed for the past three years, that was what he had prided himself on never knowing" (123–24). Such a revelation precludes a return to the prior relationship of acceptance and trust and finally leads Hassib to seek a military command, a decision that is largely an expression of his despair.

In typical Drieu fashion, the events of the story acquire, especially in the closing pages, a generalized significance that trespasses into the realms of depth psychology, an area to which Drieu chooses to give theological overtones. Although Hassib claims to be "a poet who sings of life and not a theologian indiscreetly lifting the robe of God" (96), he has in fact studied theology and learned to probe "the most fearful secrets of the human heart" (113). His inability to respect this distinction between delight in the relative and quest for the absolute—and to hold to the former—brings tragedy to his life. "Thinking of God and his absolute has made me an idiot" (204–205), he confides to Beloukia one day, and it is clearly this "divine" discontent at not occupying the place of God in Beloukia's life that issues in his destructive jealousy toward her.

The theological terms which Hassib uses to explain his jealousy suggest that he is making a statement not just about his own personality but also about the male character in general. The "coexistence" (92) with Mansour and what he often sees as "domination" by Beloukia are recognized as forming a situation that is intolerable for a man. Hassib's jealousy is consequently seen from one point of view as an assertion of a fundamental feature of the male character, destined to dissatisfaction unless it attains absolute dominance. At the same time, however, it appears as an expression of his weakness, of his inability to assert himself in sufficient measure to overcome his rivals in Beloukia's life. To this extent *Beloukia* may be seen as an extension, development, and generalization of the theme of jealousy explored in *Journal d'un homme trompé*.

The very general features that Hassib's jealousy assumes also reveal it as simply the most obvious manifestation of a pressing demand for unity. Unity obsesses Hassib but it is an ideal that he fails to achieve in his own life. Beloukia recognizes this basic element of Hassib's character on their first meeting. Here is a man capable of penetrating her being to depths which she herself has never explored. She glimpses in him the possibility of entering into a "universe" different from the one she knows, a universe in which fidelity and infidelity cease to be contradictory and merge into a unity that transcends both. She is, however, also instinctively aware of the unresolved contradictions that mark this man. His mouth, representative of his whole personality, hesitates between "a regret and a hope, a first kiss and a farewell, a promise and a threat, cruelty and gentleness, the most discreet obscenity and ironical respect" (42). Though these contradictions appear to fade under the effect of their passion, they reemerge when jealousy is aroused.

The classic conflict between thought and action also manifests itself in Hassib and constitutes a further rent in the fabric of the unified life to which he aspires. He presents himself as being "married [. . .] to the glory of both the singer and the soldier" (130), but he has a tendency to dream which, by depriving him of a sense of the concrete, threatens to disqualify him from taking an active part in public life: "He would go off dreaming through the alleys, dreaming till he lost the sense of his body. He was simply a passing cloud of images and words" (77).

Through the progressive revelation of Hassib's personality, *Beloukia* gradually sheds its exotic facade to reveal itself as another stage in Drieu's examination of the self as it manifests itself in his society. As Jean Vandal remarked in reviewing the novel shortly after publication: "Drieu cannot forget his time, he cannot forget love either. He solves the problem by sending them together to Baghdad."[5] The setting marks an interesting change in Drieu's means of expression, but the fundamental thematic approach does not vary.

Though Hassib may in the final analysis be no more than a geographically and temporally transplanted version of Gille, the person of Beloukia does represent a significant new creation in Drieu's fiction. In the richness of her character and the life she leads, Beloukia is a far cry from the major female figures of the earlier novels. With an intensity scarcely tinged by reflection, regret, or moral constraint, she eagerly embraces the varying aspects and phases of her life as they arise. In all, four men have played an important role in her life. In her youth she had given herself to a young chieftain who, overwhelmed by her beauty, had abandoned his post, carried her off, and subsequently killed himself. This incident remains deeply engraved on her memory. Her second lover, Yacoub, whose death in battle "had rent her flesh" (73), still haunts her memory because of the intensity of their relationship. Now, she remains devoted to Mansour and their children, while Hassib's love has become a necessity for her. Despite his jealousy Hassib is compelled to acknowledge the richness of Beloukia's personality and to accept the consequent demands she makes on life. Lying wounded and helpless he expresses thoughts that he has long recognized to be true: "She needs Mansour and she needs Hassib, she needs Hassan and she needs the smile of her servants, of her equerries, of her negroes, all the perfumes of Arabia, the flowers of Persia. And she scorns and remains unaware of the terrible austerity of the existence we lead" (197). Such thoughts no longer arouse his indignation, since he recognizes that she is simply remaining "faithful to the essence of her life" (196).

These words of Hassib indicate that Beloukia is for him rather more than a mistress. In her he sees a conjunction of tenderness and action, of delicate femininity and frank sensuality, of sensitivity and recognition of life's demands. She symbolizes all the richness and the unity of life which he himself is incapable of embracing except fleetingly through her. When he is closest to her, his life, "apparently rent," is described as "gathered up and reconciled beneath the sign of that princess" (157). Beloukia emerges as a symbolic semidivine figure. She not only combines the elements of Hassib's ideal woman: one who is both active mother and passive mistress; she also unifies in her person through sexual association the contradictions of Hassib's personality. It is significant that Felsan should refer to Beloukia as a "phantom" which Hassib is pursuing (188) and that in his arms Hassib should recall Beloukia as having uttered "cries that recalled and declared to him the mortal impulse of combat" (156). Beloukia provides a link for Hassib between the worlds of love and violent action.

It is in terms of this symbolic function of Beloukia that we may best explain Hassib's reluctance to take advantage of the political turmoil and get rid of his rivals Mansour and Hassan. His motivation is not simply that of pleasing his mistress. Rather he is reluctant to destroy one facet of a life whose richness and unity are psychologically so necessary for him. In particular, the role of tender mother and devoted wife—the center of a united family situation—is one that is of particular importance to him. Moreover, the saving of Mansour and Hassan may by extension be seen as an attempt by Hassib to combat the jealousy that he sees as belittling his character and making him unworthy of his mistress. By refusing to kill Mansour and Hassan he is refusing to yield to the claims of his jealousy. He wishes to dominate by generosity and bravery rather than by facile elimination and at the same time to preserve the splendid unity of his mistress's life.

The symbolic role of Beloukia is suggested quite early in the novel in the brief physical description: "Beloukia had the body of a courtesan, but the limbs of a huntress, and the head of a princess" (15). It is only at the end of the novel, however, within the context of action, that she attains her full stature, reaches "the height of her genius" (202), and expresses the perfection of Hassib's womanly ideal. In tending the wounded Hassib she recalls the maternal nurse figure that haunts Drieu's fiction. Following the flight of Mansour and the caliph to the provinces, she assumes control of the palace, in which she is besieged, and directs the defense, taking her turn with bow and lance, but also finding time to act the gentle lover. At this moment she appears considerably larger than life and suggests to Hassib a conjunction of the various idealizations of woman current in the ancient world: "That woman is all the goddesses of the Greeks; she is as inexhaustible as Venus, as faithful and inaccessible as Diana, as rational and warlike as Minerva" (216). This rather extravagant image from classical mythology is evoked by a no less extravagant and highly symbolic situation. Hassib and Beloukia are about to come together for the last time and her preparations for love recall at each stage that she is both warrior and woman: "She had loosened her belt that was heavy with a dagger and had allowed her thick dress to fall. Underneath she was naked, except for her stomach and her breasts, which were corseted with mail. She unlaced herself and, amid the iron, there reappeared for the eyes of Hassib, the breasts that he had so deeply loved and which, he knew, would presently and inexorably close themselves off again beneath this iron and beneath the gold" (216). Gradually, however, the purely feminine impulse prevails as "the warrior began to groan softly like a woman" (217).

The portrayal of the princess Beloukia is an extreme example of Drieu's apparent inability to endow his female characters with a genuine personality of their own. Drieu's women tend to become the means to a mystical experience of love rather than simply people in their own right. Despite their general importance in Drieu's work, women remain essentially an "atmosphere" or a "climate" in which men move in search of their elusive ideal. Beloukia falls clearly into this pattern, especially as the novel's exotic elements remove her further from a situation of psychological realism. She achieves reality only in Hassib's presence and through his eyes. As she makes her way to his house in the first pages of the novel she is described progressively as "silhouette," "lady," and "princess" (9–10), but she attains her full womanly stature only when she reaches his house.

In the final analysis Beloukia is important principally as a projection of Hassib's ideal self: in this woman he finds the unity that he lacks, sexual union with her becoming a means of identification with this ideal. In a moment of rapture he says to himself: "Never has a body spoken to me like the body of Beloukia. Never has the moving conjuncture of a single human body told me so much about all the fine, harmonious possibilities in the universe" (55). Such moments of union, however, are recognized as brief exceptions to a human condition from which the absolute is normally excluded. They belong to an unsullied "heaven" to which lovers naturally aspire but which only momentarily challenges the rule of the relative and mediocre.

The precarious nature of the ideal and the other-worldly aspect of the lovers' "heaven" are suggested throughout the novel by the close association between love and death. At one point, for example, Hassib and Beloukia make love in a castle "suspended over the abysses" (55). Beloukia's love for both the young chieftain and for Yacoub lies under the shadow of death and her relationship with Hassib is at its most intense when death threatens. Beloukia has a vision of Yacoub in a cemetery and this setting for the political meeting also suggests that the claims of love and political action are reconcilable only in death. Moreover, one of Hassib's last statements to Beloukia before he leaves her indicates that ultimately he recognizes the vanity of pursuing the ideal on earth: "Clearly he would have to give up looking for the absolute in life and seek it in death" (212).

In this way the novel has a level of significance that marks a new stage in Drieu's writing. It is true that the concluding pages of *Drôle de voyage* suggest a widening of Drieu's philosophy, but the whole conception of *Beloukia,* with its exotic setting, theological terminology, mythological imagery, and especially its "cosmic" dimension, sets this novel apart. Without abandoning the psychological penetration of his earlier works, Drieu, like Malraux in his novels of the same decade, introduces with *Beloukia* a breadth of perspective that announces the more complex novels that immediately follow.

Résumé

Examination of Drieu's literature of imagination in the early 1930s shows the period as one in which a conscious effort is made principally in two areas. On the one hand Drieu seeks to take stock of ideas previously expressed in his literature and to re-present them both more precisely and in broader, more acceptable perspective. On the other hand he uses this period of reflection to refine his literary technique. *Drôle de voyage* is clearly more than a successful rewriting of *L'Homme couvert de femmes,* but it does serve to elaborate and clarify in rather more objective fashion the fictional character of Gille introduced in the earlier novel. *Drôle de voyage* is considered by some critics as Drieu's most accomplished novel and few would deny that the integration of the various psychological, sociological, and philosophical elements that it contains is handled with a competence that shows a writer at the height of his powers. The short stories of *La Comédie de Charleroi* and *Journal d'un homme trompé* equally show a considerable development of technique from those of *Plainte contre inconnu.* Eminently readable, they display a range of points of view and a mastery of subject matter that find them a place among Drieu's best works. Indeed, many critics class *La Comédie de Charleroi* as Drieu's finest literary achievement. The two collections of short stories also allow Drieu to give a more considered presentation of attitudes to war and man-woman relationships. Although *La Comédie de Charleroi* is written in the first person and contains some intensely lyrical passages, it is much less intensely personal in tone than the poems of *Interrogation* and constitutes Drieu's clearest statement on modern warfare. *Journal d'un homme trompé* is likewise Drieu's fullest investigation of man-woman relationships in contemporary society.

Despite the evident similarities between Hassib and Gille, *Beloukia,* written in the mid-1930s, stands somewhat apart from the three earlier works. *Beloukia* not only introduces a new exotic element which broadens Drieu's fictional field; it also brings a new perspective to the analysis of the self. Through the introduction of the idealized figure of the princess Beloukia, further aspects of the male self are revealed and tensions grow as the choice between love and action, announced at the end of *Drôle de voyage,* becomes more pressing. This relatively new approach announced in *Beloukia* will find fuller expression in *L'Homme à cheval* [The Man on Horseback] some six years later and is perhaps also apparent in the latter pages of *Gilles.*

Chapter Five
The Polyphonic Novels

Rêveuse bourgeoisie

With the completion of *Rêveuse bourgeoisie* [Dreamy Bourgeoisie] in 1937 Drieu believed he had reached a new stage of literary maturity. He is reported to have spoken of it as "my first novel, I mean the first novel to count for me." By comparison with this work, his earlier novels were, he felt, if not "frivolous," at least limited to "subjects that were rather slight."[1] Although it is always dangerous to take Drieu's remarks about his writings at their face value—and the existence of such novels as *Drôle de voyage, Le Feu follet,* and *Blèche* is sufficient proof of the undue harshness of his words—such remarks about *Rêveuse bourgeoisie* at least serve to focus attention on the wide perspective that the work embraces. It is, as Pol Vandromme remarked, "the novel of a society"[2] since in it we have Drieu's vision of certain aspects of French society during the period of roughly thirty-five years from the early 1890s. The problems associated with a conviction of social decadence and with the place of the individual within this situation remain central, but the historical perspective gives them a new depth.

The five parts of *Rêveuse bourgeoisie* follow the fortunes of three generations of a middle class family. In Part I the attitudes of a section of the late-nineteenth-century French bourgeoisie are mediated principally through Ernest and Blanche Ligneul. The Ligneuls are prosperous Parisians anxious to add dignity to their wealth by marrying off their daughter Agnès to someone with a particle to his name. Such social snobbery overcomes their misgivings about certain aspects of the life-style of Camille Le Pesnel, the son of an old-established Norman family now practicing as a lawyer in Paris, and a marriage is contracted. Parts II and III trace the progressive collapse of Camille as one after another of the business projects he initiates fail through his naiveté or incompetence. He plunges deeper and deeper into debt, calling more and more frequently on his rich father-in-law for help. As Camille's financial situation deteriorates, so his emotional dependence on his mistress, Rose Renard, increases. This fact, together with his inability to provide financial security for his wife and two children, places considerable strains on the marriage.

The final two parts of the novel deal more specifically with the third generation: Yves and Geneviève, the children of Agnès and Camille. At the beginning of Part IV Geneviève reveals herself as the narrator of the story and it is she who tells of the deaths of Agnès, Camille, and her brother. Yves, in despair at seeing the development in himself of those characteristics of his father that he most detests, volunteers for military service in Morocco. With the coming of World War I he returns to Europe to die in battle. Genevieve herself, with the strength and persistency that characterize only the women in this novel, lives through the crises of the family and appears largely successful in overcoming what Yves sees as the fatality of his heredity. In the closing pages she announces that she is expecting a baby, and in this event she sees the possibility of renewed hope: "It will be something, something unexpected. Something which opens up a divine path of tremendous hope" (535).

Geneviève's maternal grandmother is one of the work's most fascinating and complex characters. She is, it appears, influenced and to some degree bound by the narrow perspectives of her financially successful husband and by the intriguing old priest l'abbé Maurois. However, despite a certain adaptation to the bourgeois values that they profess, she retains a vitality that prevents her from lapsing into total conformity. Such qualities make her, at least in the eyes of her daughter's suitor, Gustave Ganche, "the most vital person in the whole family" (309).

The redeeming features of Blanche Ligneul's personality, those that may be seen as an instinctive protest against the social world in which she lives, are suggested in the portrait painted of her in the opening pages of the novel. While she remains "appropriately dressed" with all the accepted attire of her class: flower-bedecked hat, parasol, corset, and flounced dress, she mutters against the restrictions that such articles impose on her movement and gives the impression of a woman "for whom coquetry has never existed" (11). Similar attitudes inform her religious observance. Although she never thinks of questioning the beliefs and standards in which she has been raised, she brings to her religious practice a candor that contrasts with the Establishment-oriented clergy. She is instinctively repelled by the modern unaesthetic lines of the church into which she slips on the way to the beach, and she dislikes the musty "priestly" smell of the abbé Maurois's residence with its suggestions of intrigue. Moreover, her brief, ingenuous prayer, in which modesty and self-effacement mingle a little incongruously with mild self-satisfaction at her husband's business successes, indicates that she has only partly fallen victim to the middle-class sophistication of Paris.

Blanche Ligneul is, however, sufficiently bourgeois to be afflicted by a tendency to dream, a characteristic which the author associates with her social class and which gives the novel its title. As elsewhere in Drieu's works, such a tendency to dream is seen as a wistful longing by the bourgeoisie for a world of action and adventure which it is no longer capable of embracing. Consequently the "dreaminess" of the bourgeoisie is seen to have both positive and negative aspects. On the one hand it is a reminder of a past age of vigorous action that still exerts its fascination; on the other hand it bears witness to the bourgeoisie's present inability to act with vigor, thus constituting a compensatory flight to a world of insubstantial imaginings. So it is that Blanche Ligneul encourages in her grandson a keen admiration of Napoleon and his world, is attracted by the prospect of travel to exotic lands, and vaguely pictures her daughter marrying a sailor or explorer whose adventures she may experience vicariously. Such dreams never leave the realm of thought, but their existence at least indicates that, despite the bourgeois life she leads, Blanche Ligneul has not altogether lost the sense of action, adventure, and risk that marked her forebears.

Ernest Ligneul, by contrast, lacks the imagination to assert himself even vicariously elsewhere than in his abstract world of figures and balance sheets. All his initiative and energy are directed to working in his office and making money, and he is almost totally lacking in positive qualities in the area of human relations. The narrator remarks that "M. Ligneul would lose his composure when confronted by a woman, a man, anyone of whatever rank or whatever personality" (113). Indeed, it is to this constant timidity, to this refusal to assert himself when confronted with a problem involving living beings, that his family misfortunes are attributed.

Within the context of this novel—and also within the framework of Drieu's general ideas on social decadence—Ernest Ligneul comes to represent those life-denying, dehumanizing qualities that spell disaster in interpersonal relations between man and man or man and woman. The consequences of his inability to assert himself as head of a household are that his sexual relations with his wife are characterized by difficulty and weakness and that at no stage is he able to give his daughter an attractive example of manliness. Suspicious of those who are in the field of "letters" with its insistence on the human, and preferring the antiseptic, abstract world of "figures," Ernest Ligneul is depicted as having completely lost contact with the soil, the source of man's physical and moral strength. In consequence, close relationships with his fellow beings prove impossible.

This fearful businessman is, however, not lacking in drive. His business success is the result of persistence and intense effort, precisely those qualities whose absence he deplores in his son-in-law. Such vigor and vitality are, as it were, his inheritance from a past, more heroic era, paralleling in many respects his wife's romantic fancies. The following generations of his family find difficulty in exerting themselves even to this extent.

The other members of this first generation depicted in the novel are of quite a different order from M. and Mme Ligneul. Camille's parents and his perceptive old aunt Yvonne have remained buried in their native Normandy, relatively impervious to the modernizing tendencies that tourism brings ever more insistently from Paris. The description of Camille's family home illustrates the attitudes and the situation of his parents: "The small house had not changed; it was now buried amid an accumulation of grotesque chalets" (377). Though progressively swamped by the sophisticated vulgarity of the modern world, M. and Mme Le Pesnel keep their roots firmly set in their native Norman soil.

Mme Le Pesnel remains in the background as a self-effacing farmer's wife, content with her humble lot. Her husband, though rarely seen and then only briefly described, emerges in much greater relief as a personification of those rural virtues whose disappearance Drieu's Gille figures, at least in their romantic moments, deeply regret. Whenever visitors arrive he is found in clogs working in his garden or reading Greek or Latin classics in the original, reluctant to be drawn out of this environment into one which, perhaps only half-consciously, he despises. It is significant that Blanche Ligneul is attracted to such a man.

Aunt Yvonne holds similar attitudes, but her perspicacity is far greater than that of her male relation. She mercilessly cuts through Camille's cant and hypocrisy when he returns in search of money and proposes a clear course of action which contrasts with her nephew's lack of drive in his business "initiatives."

The presentation of the first of the generations consequently covers a wide spectrum of social attitudes and shows different stages and aspects of what is seen as social decline. The values represented by those members of the Le Pesnel family who have resisted the temptation to uproot themselves and adapt to modern urban life are considered admirable but progressively more difficult to maintain and finally doomed to extinction. It is no accident that all M. Le Pesnel's direct female relations in Normandy, including his daughter Sophie, are unmarried. By the end of the novel there is in this region no heir to the Le Pesnel name. The Ligneuls, on the other hand, having at least partially succumbed to "that madness which contorts thousands of weak beings and directs them to the ambition of the cities" (378), clearly belong to the modern bourgeoisie. Each, however, retains certain strengths or human qualities that complement one another and enable them to survive in the Babylon that is Paris. Such strength is singularly lacking in their chosen son-in-law.

Camille has cut his ties irrevocably with the world of his parents, but the transition to Paris has proved too sudden for adequate social and psychological adjustment. He finds himself still vaguely nostalgic for his father's way of life, which invariably has such a salutary effect on him when he returns to visit. He is, for example, proud of his "rather rough and virile childhood among fishermen's children and young English boys and girls" (38). On the other hand, he aspires to the professional competence and business acumen of Ernest Ligneul without possessing the requisite single-mindedness and independence. In short, Camille is a Barresian *déraciné,* depicted as weak because lost between two incompatible worlds and hence lacking the qualities of success in either. He is probably Drieu's best literary portrait of Watteau's painting from which the Gille characters take their name. It is significant, moreover, that he should return to his Norman birthplace to spend there the last days of his life.

Perhaps the most obvious psychological manifestation of Camille's incapacity to adapt to urban ways is his inability to make contact in any meaningful way with the reality before him. His tendency to what is termed from time to time "absent-mindedness" (38) often prevents him from perceiving at all what is before his eyes. It is not until the arrangements for the marriage are virtually concluded and the Le Pesnels have come to visit the Ligneuls at Paris that he becomes properly conscious of Agnès's reality (121). On this occasion he details with considerable surprise some of her attractive physical features. Such revelations of the real are rare in Camille's consciousness. Indeed the dreaminess that life in Paris has produced in him has brought such confusion to his mind that the world of his imagination at times assumes greater reality for him than the one in which his body moves. As Gustave Ganche remarks to Agnès: "He has discovered a particular way of deluding himself about things that are overwhelming in their reality by deceiving himself about the value of the projects that he is constantly conceiving" (300). Agnès herself later has the opportunity to confirm the truth of this remark when Camille tries to convince her of the viability of one of his planned business undertakings. As he elaborates this fiction of his mind it attains such reality for him that it is as though it had been suggested by someone else. It is for reasons of this kind that Camille becomes such a pathetic figure. What little imagination he does have tends to be focused on the easy acquisition of money, the very area in which by nature he is incapable of success. "His imaginative powers never issued in action. For him money seemed to be something that was both near at hand and very distant and which depended solely on luck and not on effort" (63).

Camille thus has none of the qualities that serve to redeem the previous generation of his wife's parents. He lacks the drive of Ernest Ligneul and also the romantic imagination of Blanche Ligneul, both of which qualities, albeit in a perverted fashion, illustrate continuing contact with a less decadent age. Camille is quite simply lost and weak, provoking the derision of his business colleagues and retaining no authority or respect in his family. He is one of the myriad modern city-dwellers described, in an overt political reference, as "those who, left to their own devices, are incapable of anything, but who would have contributed a great deal to a master or to a definite code of conduct" (350).

There is, however, one situation in which Camille is able to achieve contact with the reality which so eludes him: in the arms of his working-class mistress, Rose Renard. Only with her does he have a sense of personal authenticity and strength, and only on her breast does his hand, normally stretching after the insubstantial clouds of fanciful ambition, arrive at a consciousness of its own reality. In her person Rose unites and reconciles those contradictions that rend Camille's personality: in a litany of praise he extols her as "this daughter of the fields, [who] is also a delicate Parisian" (388). Elsewhere she is described as "vigorous and maternal" (155), the combination of Amazon and mother that tends to characterize Drieu's idealized female figures. In her he finds a refuge from his failures in a world to which he cannot adapt.

Geneviève proclaims her father as a "victim of love" (497) and there is evidence in the last pages of the novel that she harbors a reluctant admiration for his continued devotion to Rose. She even attributes such feelings to her mother: "[Agnès] was admirably aware of what was best in Camille, that quality which, when all is said and done, explains him and completely justifies him: his love for Rose" (532). In the expression of such sentiments we have a further example of the perspicacity of the women characters of this novel. Instinctively recognizing that Camille's sensuality constitutes his only possible link with reality, they are prepared to condone his relationship with the only woman capable of allowing it adequate expression.

Agnès Ligneul is one of the many young women in Drieu's fiction to be seen as victims of their bourgeois education and family upbringing. Quite devoid of independent imagination, Agnès brings to her marriage with Camille all the standards and prejudices with which she has grown up. In the union itself, for example, she sees an equality which satisfies the demands of marriage as conceived by her class: Camille is to bring to the relationship the prestige of an aristocratic name, while she brings money and an acceptable education. Questions of personal compatibility scarcely arise. Her ignorance of men is virtually total, as it is of the world outside the narrow confines of her family and Neuilly convent where she had received her schooling.

What makes Agnès a pitiable rather than a pathetic character is that below the veneer of her bourgeois upbringing, which, throughout her life, monopolizes her consciousness, are strong personal qualities awaiting expression. In the period leading up to the marriage there are glimpses of genuine passion that betray the existence of a latent sensuality. Indeed, the extent to which this manifests itself mystifies and fascinates her mother, while the narrator remarks that her desire is one of the few things that escape the "vanity" of the situation. These glimmerings of authenticity and independence, however, expressed through sensuality, remain at the stage of unfulfilled promise. She is caught in the labyrinth of her society's values and is encouraged to stay in this prison by her husband, who is willing to prostitute himself for the sake of her money. The narrator remarks: "There had been strength in her and it had all amounted to nothing. Her passion had fallen back upon her and buried her" (511).

As these latter words of Geneviève may suggest, Agnès is ultimately redeemed, at least in the eyes of her daughter, by the strength of her sensuality, expressed through a constantly frustrated devotion to her husband. Even Gustave Ganche recognizes that she is "controlled by the flesh, and that was really the only way she could be controlled" (337). Acting on this belief, he is almost successful in seducing her. Agnès, however, with the persistence that may be the only positive aspect of the prejudices of her upbringing, continues to seek emotional support from Camille, even though this fundamental need is expressed in an alienating fashion: "He was her support. She supported herself on him by means of abuse" (304).

Despite the tragedy of their marital situation, Agnès and Camille have numerous features in common. Incapable of aggressive self-assertion issuing in decisive action, they are both held in thrall by a mindless respect for money and to a lesser extent social status. The positive features of their personalities, those that have managed to escape the deadening effects of a bourgeois environment, are in both cases expressed in terms of their sensuality. In their other relationships within the social structure they are fundamentally weak and dependent creatures, easily exploited but capable of being creatively led.

The other, relatively minor, representatives of the second generation, Le Loreur and Gustave Ganche, are the spiritual sons of Ernest Ligneul. Like Agnès's father, they have adapted to the ways of modern urban bourgeois society and have attained a high degree of success. Both make persistent efforts to exploit Camille's financial troubles to seduce Agnès, but their failure reflects their incapacity in human relations. Exploitation is in fact the secret of their social and economic success and sets them apart as a different "race" from those that remain ingenuous like Camille and Agnès. In speaking of Camille's partner Gravier, Geneviève refers in the following terms to these two fundamental groups produced by modern society: "A race which is ignorant of guile, of daring, of gain, of a goal to be reached, and which stands there, gaping at the walls, after gaping for centuries at the trees and the crows, with an innocence that was less hazardous. There is another race of men set beside that one: it acts with precision and speed and exploits the former without ever allowing itself to be diverted by curiosity or pity" (351).

The announcement at the beginning of the novel's fourth part that the events are being recounted by Geneviève, a member of the third generation of the Le Pesnel–Ligneul family, introduces a sudden change of perspective. In the first place, not only is the illusion of authorial omniscience destroyed; even the impression of historicity is called into question, since it is now apparent that the narrator has been recounting what occurred during her early childhood and even before her birth. The events of the first three parts, which constitute almost three-quarters of the novel, come to be seen as a personal reconstruction of the past and hence of quite dubious authenticity. In the second place, attention is specifically directed away from the two central characters, Camille and Agnès, whose principal role in the novel is now presented as enabling Geneviève to achieve greater self-understanding. When she reveals herself as narrator, Geneviève says of the first three parts of the novel: "All that was to get to the stage of speaking of myself and Yves" (395). In one short sentence the story of Agnès, Camille, and their parents is relegated to the status of mere introduction.

This rupture in the fabric of the novel corresponds closely to the profound change in perspective from the generation of Agnès and Camille and their parents to that of their children. Geneviève reminds us that "it is given to the child to know more than its parents since it has observed them" (530), but in this case the increase in awareness is extreme. While Geneviève presents herself and her brother as becoming progressively more aware of the grim destiny of their family, and in consequence seeking to react against it, Agnès and Camille together with their parents are depicted as dumb animals led to slaughter, unconscious victims of a situation they cannot comprehend. This heightened awareness in the younger generation—the generation of Drieu's Gille-figure—is viewed in extremely positive terms: it becomes the means of "forcing on" the cycle of decadence in their own lives so that subsequent renewal and rebirth may appear. At this point, moreover, the rhythm of the narrative quickens: in this novel Drieu's cyclical theories on decadence are given expression not just thematically but also structurally.

Yves's means of "forcing on" the cycle of decadence is to degrade himself in his own eyes and in the eyes of others by exaggerating those features of his father that he most detests but which he is bitterly conscious of inheriting. Convinced that he is unworthy of Emmy Maindron, a girl of wealthy family who is in love with him, Yves goes to considerable lengths to bring his conduct into conformity with the low opinion he has of himself as Camille's son, and in so doing to excite Emmy's disgust and scorn. His frustration at being unable to shed the fatality of his family's destiny is expressed in a desire to destroy the relationship that is dearest to him. "I had to perform some ignoble act that I would tell her about and which would allow her to hate me" (470), he says to his sister. His failure in his political science examination, in which many thought he would be placed first, is, one suspects, also to be attributed to such psychological conflict. Finally, his decision to volunteer for military service in Africa is taken in the belief and in the hope that he will not return. As she witnesses this process of self-destruction, Geneviève feels that she is "slowly slipping into a common grave" (483) being dug by the surviving male member of the family.

The ways in which Geneviève seeks personal authenticity are less extreme than those of her brother. They do, however, reflect a comparable desire to plumb the depths of the lie that she, through her family, has been living and face the consequences of such a revelation. With Yves she believes that between the Maindrons and the Le Pesnels there is "a fearful moral desert" (475), and she takes bitter delight in manifesting this moral distance. Following Yves's example, she breaks with Emmy Maindron's brother, who admires her, and also follows Yves to war, where she serves as a nurse. In contrast to her brother she survives the war and, although separated from her parents, tends to lapse back into certain of the patterns that had characterized their life. At the time of Agnès's death, awareness that she remains a Le Pesnel returns: "I lapsed right back into my childhood, into the fatality of the Le Pesnels that I had completely forgotten. [. . .] I was utterly astonished and terrified to see that I had never ceased being at the mercy of my past" (510–11). Geneviève is left some money by her mother, but it is significant that it is only when this last remaining part of the money accumulated by Ernest Ligneul is spent that Geneviève is able to adopt a way of life that permits her both to live out the fatality of her identity as a Le Pesnel and at the same time to affirm her authenticity. On the suggestion of her lover, Edouard Nicorps, she becomes an actress.

Geneviève becomes aware of her likeness to Camille by gazing into a mirror, but in the theater she is enabled to manifest publicly this ineradicable similarity. The theater is an illusion—a lie—and as such is an appropriate profession for the daughter of Camille, whose life is a history of pretense and prevarication. "Actors, the Le Pesnels" (524), remarks Geneviève at one stage. But the theater is a *patent* lie and is capable of deceiving the spectator only to the extent that he is prepared to enter the world of illusion being presented. In this situation the actor or actress retains a paradoxical authenticity precisely because the illusion being lived out is conscious and obvious at every moment to whoever cares to withdraw his "suspended disbelief." "My profession is to lie and to remain truthful" (534), Geneviève claims. In this way, by becoming an actress, she is enabled consciously and deliberately to live out her destiny as a child of Camille—to press awareness of this aspect of her "self"—but at the same time to achieve authenticity. "Now, as a professional actor, I was freed from the bad conscience of those who are 'actors without being aware of it'" (524). This is her positive answer to the question she asks herself about her relationship to her father: "The question is not: have I or have I not his vices? but: will his vices be my virtues?" (530). By consciously choosing a profession which reflects her vision of herself, she is following the path of her brother and preparing the way for a more authentic future. The manner in which she is enabled to acknowledge her resemblance to Camille and to transcend it is given figurative expression in the image: "In the mirror our faces, having been brought together again, are once more parted. This time it will be for good. Not because of death, but because I am fully immersed in my life" (552).

Through the perspective of Yves and Geneviève, who together represent the generation born in the 1890s, *Rêveuse bourgeoisie* emerges as a further stage in Drieu's quest for personal authenticity in an abhorrent society by which the self is necessarily conditioned. The particular thematic contribution of the novel is its vision of the past generations with whose moral legacy the individual has to cope. The fatality of one's heredity and the need for personal authenticity are the two main emphases of the last two parts of the novel and it is the reconciliation of these two that both Yves and Geneviève desperately try to achieve. By focusing upon the historical aspects of the individual's conditioning—even though the historicity is seen as largely illusory—Drieu is able to go beyond the limited approach of previous novels, which do not seek to transcend the lifetime of the individual presented. In consequence fuller illumination is given not only to the individual's understanding of himself, but also to his understanding of the society in which he lives. In the characterization of *Rêveuse bourgeoisie* there is in fact a tendency to pass from the particular to the general, as individuals are pictured first as members of a particular family and then as representative of social groups and tendencies. As we have seen, Camille and Gustave Ganche belong to different "races" and Geneviève is aware how many Camilles populate Paris: "God knows Paris is filled with such characters. Its streets are full of that race of country folk who arrived dreaming in broad daylight and who, not being bitten by any precisely formulated ambition, never wake up and sometimes continue like this for several generations" (351). Moreover, in the context of Geneviève's choice of the theater, Paris is described as "a theater where five million second-rate actors from the four corners of the provinces hang on desperately" (523).

Structurally the work is extremely interesting in that the form it takes poses some of the fundamental problems that inform Drieu's fiction. Especially significant is the introduction of a narrator who is one of the actors in the story but whose vision of the situation that determines her personality and character is partial and largely imagined. In this way Drieu gives not just thematic but formal expression to his continuing problem of how the individual in a society can achieve an authentic view of himself and of the society by which he is determined. Drieu could have structured his novel rather more traditionally by introducing his narrator as Camus introduced Rieux in *La Peste* [The Plague]. In Camus's novel nothing is described that is outside the knowledge and experience of the doctor, so that the illusion of historicity and authenticity is preserved. It is significant that the work is classified by Camus as a "chronicle." *Rêveuse bourgeoisie*, however, is more ambitious in structural conception than *La Peste*. By identifying the historical reconstruction of an individual's family as largely projection or myth, Drieu calls into question the very possibility of the individual's ever having anything but a partial understanding of the historical process that makes him and his society what they are.

On the other hand, imaginatively conceived myth and projection at least constitute a standard—albeit one that is subject to revision—that enables some perspective on the present. A certain view of one's origins enables one to act and react in something more than a mere void. Myths of golden or heroic ages in the past, and perhaps even devotion to tradition, have no other explanation. In *Rêveuse bourgeoisie* belief in a certain heredity enables Geneviève and possibly also Yves to react against the bourgeois dreaminess that they observe at work in themselves. In their different ways they seek the elusive ideal self that they can now identify with a previous stage of the cycle of history in which they conceive themselves to be locked. With a conviction born of the vision that she has presented of her family, Geneviève expresses this hope: "I am sure that in the lineage of our ancestors, apart from Grandmother, there are some who preferred us, Yves or me—and probably both of us together, for we really were the brother and the sister. Those are the ones that are our true parents. It was imperative for me to cling to them in order to tolerate and fight Camille" (529).

Gilles

The appearance in 1939 of *Gilles,* the longest and most ambitious novel Drieu wrote, brought to a close an important stage in his literary career. It is, as Frédéric Grover remarks,[3] a *roman bilan* ("novel of summation") in that, within the framework of one novel, it gathers together many of the significant themes and character types that had been treated previously. This is particularly true of the principal character, whose "plural" Christian name draws attention to the fact that he represents a "summation" of the "Gille" figures of earlier novels and short stories. *Gilles* may also be seen as completing a diptych of society initiated by *Rêveuse bourgeoisie.* Despite a considerable change in authorial perspective, the novel continues and concludes a picture of modern society begun with the presentation of the Ligneul–Le Pesnel family in the early 1890s. Gilles is, as it were, a resurrected Yves, one who has survived the purification brought by death in battle, and who lives on, "bearing the stigma of Cain" (155), to face the task of adapting to the decadence of the postwar years. *Gilles* covers the years from 1917 to the Spanish Civil War. It provides a particular perspective on a number of the major political and literary events that marked a period which, as Drieu had prophesied, came to a violent end with the outbreak of the Second World War. In consequence, the novel gives a privileged view of the two major aspects of Drieu's fiction: the presentation and castigation of a society considered as irremediably decadent and the portrayal of a particular individual seeking a way to adapt to the social circumstances of his age.

The first of the four parts of the novel, "La Permission" [Leave], evokes the problems and the temptations of a young soldier spending his leave among the bright lights and luxury of Paris. Fresh from the dangers of front-line fighting, which both terrifies him and attracts him, Gilles Gambier wanders the streets of the capital where shops and women subtly beckon. The attractive images that flash before his disoriented eyes are admirably communicated by a series of short, often disjointed sentences that serve to place these early pages among Drieu's most evocative writing:

> Finally he allowed himself to look, to desire. All these people, regarded with contempt for long months, seemed strange to him. Perhaps he detested the men, but he was looking only at the women whom he adored. It was a mild evening. If he had looked at the sky, something he used to do at the front but which he immediately forgot to do in the big city which diverts all man's senses to a few fetishes, he would have seen a charming sky. A starless Parisian sky. It was a mild evening slightly tinged with cold. The women were beginning to open their furs. They were looking at him. Working girls or street girls. The street girls tempted him more than the working girls, but he wanted to play with his desire until he ground his teeth or fainted. Everybody seemed to be making for a particular goal. And he too had a goal the shape of which was still unclear to him. Sooner or later that shape was going to reveal itself. (17)

The final words of this passage suggest that the aimlessness of Gilles's sortie into Parisian society, into "the land of women" (15) as he initially describes it, is only apparent. His failure to look above his present surroundings into the night sky, associated as this is with the front line, indicates that already he is at least half-consciously seeking an entry into this society from which his better nature recoils in disgust. Shortly afterwards he introduces himself into the wealthy Falkenberg family, pays court to the daughter of the house, Myriam, and finally marries her in the full expectation that the union will not last.

Gilles's visit to Paris is not merely the brief respite from the rigors of war that the title of the first part suggests. Because of the influence and connections of the Falkenberg family and thanks to a war wound, Gilles is kept out of front-line fighting, gains access to an elevated stratum of bourgeois society, and subsequently comes into contact with certain aspects of the political life of the Third Republic.

The most significant comment on the society of the time to be mediated by Gilles's initial experience of Paris is found in the description of Mr. Falkenberg. A Jew, and hence for Gilles a typical representative of modern bourgeois society, Myriam's father is a wealthy businessman. Like Ernest Ligneul, to whose generation he belongs, all his energies have been directed to the making of money, which is important to him as a sign of success. Now that his business activity has ceased and his two sons, killed in the war, are unable to continue the activity that has given meaning to his life, Mr. Falkenberg is faced with the sterility of his existence: "Mr. Falkenberg believed in nothingness. He believed in nothingness as he had believed in money. For him the universe was a Stock Exchange flanked by a nursery; all around there was nothingness" (119). Through this man Drieu presents the moral bankruptcy of a whole society, one which places abstractions and dead objects above the living realities of the world and remains indifferent to "sky, colors, smells, women, children, people, God's terrible presence everywhere in countless gods" (118).

Such life-denying attitudes are reflected also in Myriam, who emerges as one of the best drawn but most pitiable of Drieu's fictional female characters. From her father she acquires a sense of the importance of money and social standing, and, like Agnès Ligneul, she is naive enough to believe that these contributions that she brings to the union with Gilles will serve to bind him to her and will replace the human qualities that he needs. It is for this reason that on several occasions Gilles refers to Myriam as an "accomplice" in the crime that he commits in marrying her. Through Myriam, Drieu also launches an attack on certain of the educational tendencies of the age, notably the stress on feminism. There is in Myriam a masculinity which Gilles deplores. "Who would want to have anything to do with a girl so lacking in femininity, intuition, and coquetry, one so sexually unresponsive?" (133), he muses immediately after the marriage.

Numerous political references are to be found in "La Permission," and Gilles himself makes contact with several important figures, but it is not until the long second part, entitled "L'Elysée," that aspects of the political life of the Third Republic receive particular emphasis. The presentation of the Révolte group under the leadership of Caël—an obvious fictional transposition of André Breton and the Surrealists—also introduces a view oı the literary life of the time and its relationship to politics.

"L'Elysée" is dotted with forthright bitter denunciations of leading political and avant-garde literary figures of the day. Caël, for example, is "a charlatan" (177) and his movement a "nest of snakes" (183), while the President of the Republic, Mr. Morel (who represents Millerand) is stated to be fearful, indecisive, and hypocritical. For the most part, however, Drieu prefers to present his condemnation of these aspects of contemporary social life in less direct fashion. For example, to convey his vision of the French political world he centers his attention on Paul Morel, the president's weak son, who provides a link between the Elysée palace and Caël's band. Furthermore, he tends to give prominence to certain apparently trivial events and snatches of conversation which convey a general atmosphere rather than baldly state a point of view. These indirect methods finally provide a more convincing indication of social values than the polemics in which Gilles is from time to time tempted to indulge.

The eighteen-year-old Paul Morel is not only a central figure in the structure of "L'Elysée"; he is also seen as representative of many of the tendencies of the society in which he is so utterly lost. As Caël and his band are aware, Paul Morel is easily exploited. He is scandalized by his father's acceptance of the presidency of the Third Republic and in consequence seeks to dissociate himself from the social conformism that the position demands. With such attitudes he is an easy prey to the overtures of Galant and Caël, who, for their part, are anxious to use him to destroy his father. Gilles feels considerable sympathy for Paul Morel as an individual—and indeed he is the only one of Paul's associates to make a serious effort to help him—but he remains in Gilles's eyes the typical offspring of the leading family in a decadent political and social system. During an interview with President Morel and his wife, Gilles is led to consider the whole Morel family and in particular the mother, who had given birth to Paul and his loose, opium-smoking sister Antoinette: "He gazed at the woman from whom all that misery had come. She, like so many others, was only a channel through which it passed" (313). This and many other references scattered through the novel indicate that the nervous debility which finally leads Paul to suicide is symptomatic of an illness that is widespread in the society that his father nominally leads. With no firm leader or values to follow and assailed on all sides by those who would profit from his emotional instability, Paul stumbles from one unscrupulous "friend" to another, finding nowhere except in Gilles the human values for which he only half-consciously craves. He is one of the general run of pitiable beings of which society, for the Fascist-inclined Gilles, is principally composed: those who are "weak but obsessed by the idea of strength" (292).

Gilles is especially sensitive to Paul Morel's plight since he instinctively feels that this young adolescent, lost in an alien society, is at bottom a kindred spirit. But for the education he had received at the hands of his old Norman mentor, Carentan, far from Paris, Gilles sees himself as being just as desperately lost in society as Paul. In this way Paul Morel forms a bridge between Gilles and the rest of society. Through him Gilles is enabled to establish the extent to which his own sense of personal inadequacy is typical of those whom he observes and this serves to confirm him in his general views on social and political decadence.

The presence of Paul Morel in the pages of "L'Elysée" also serves to illuminate the shallowness of the Révolte group and the insincerity of the beliefs they so vociferously proclaim. Attracted by Caël's call to violent action (Breton's famous words: "the only interesting act, is to go down into the street with a revolver and to fire at random until there is no one left" are directly attributed to Caël [189]) but, unaware that such verbal extravagance cloaks a fundamental sense of weakness, Paul determines to murder his father. Panic-stricken that anyone should ever take it into his head to act upon their calls to violence, Caël and Galant frantically try to locate their protégé to dissuade him from precisely the act that they themselves have encouraged him to conceive:

> Caël, who, in his writings had often spoken of murders, of revolvers, who had despatched to a theoretical massacre all the bourgeoisie, the army, the clergy, the government, the teaching profession, the Academy and many other entities, contemplated, haggard-eyed, the sudden possibility of blood. Above all he was terrified at getting mixed up in this affair. (303)

Caël and his colleagues are seen to have as little real contact with reality—the capacity to "bite into reality" (248), as Drieu expresses it—as the young man whose projected action represents his last desperate attempt to attain such contact.

Despite Gilles's conviction of the mediocrity of the Révolte group, he frequents its members and attends their activities because they constitute for him one of the few remaining efforts to dislocate and destroy a tottering social structure: "He was joining these destroyers out of despair, because the little strength that he saw around him was to be found only in destruction" (191). This belief in the inevitability, and indeed the desirability, of the destruction and subsequent transformation of contemporary society informs all the pages of *Gilles,* but it is focused most specifically in the third section, appropriately entitled "L'Apocalypse." This section illustrates the collapse of a whole society, from which Gilles progressively distances himself. France is seen as a country that is "without government, headless, but which, with all its intestinal mass, drowned in fat, was stifling its heart" (441). Such a vision of a country at the point of death is inspired principally by two political events: the congress of the Radical party presided over by Jules Chanteau (Edouard Herriot) at Château-le-roi and the riots of February 1934 associated with the Stavisky affair.[4]

The restrained verbal violence of Gilles's attack on the anachronistic Radical party in the central chapter of "L'Apocalypse" provides some of Drieu's most vivid writing. Snatches of conversation and brief excerpts from the speeches of the party leaders mingle with perceptive remarks and unsympathetic descriptions of the participants' physical appearance from the uninvolved observer that Gilles now feels himself to be. Gilbert de Clérences makes a valiant effort to hide his own insufficiencies and to convince the party of the need for new attitudes and new policies. Chanteau, however, determined to prevent his party from entering the world of the twentieth century, soon quashes such dangerous thoughts: "Chanteau, giving a broad display of his paunch, came forward on the stage that had witnessed so many of his triumphs. With the same tragicomical movement he had been coming forward like this each year since the war, on this national stage" (406–407). This use of images and vocabulary drawn from the theater to portray the sham and pretense that characterize political and social life of the time is an aspect of Drieu's literary technique that he also uses skillfully in other sections of the novel.

The congress of the Radical party also serves Gilles as a focus for an attack on the narrow Rationalism which he sees as sapping the vitality of his country. For him the twentieth century is the age of Nietzsche (381), an age of methods rather than doctrines (391), in which a frankly recognized will to power must be allowed to reconstruct society on the "harsh, cruel foundations of the possible" (382). It has been misled for too long by Rationalistic political schemes and the unrealistic utopias that they engender: "An end had to be put to all these absurd pretensions of rationalism, of the philosophy of the enlightenment" (382).

The excitement, tension, and distress produced in Paris by the Stavisky riots are communicated in the closing pages of "L'Elysée" through the particular experience that Gilles has of them. Quite unexpectedly he becomes involved in the events of February 6 and is quick to interpret them as a movement of national significance, indicative of a profound desire in the people for revival and regeneration. War memories feed his enthusiasm at being involved in action and his imagination takes charge: "In a moment he was transfigured. Looking to his right and his left, he saw himself surrounded once again by the divine couple, Fear and Courage, which presides in time of war. Its fiery whips cracked" (433). For the first time since the war he feels that he is really living because he is involved in a vigorous popular reaction against the system that he wishes to destroy. The forces of conservatism, however, are allowed to reestablish control and the stage is set for the ill-starred Popular Front to come into being. Gilles, for his part, finally makes a political commitment and embraces fascism.

The last political and social situation to be treated in *Gilles* is of quite a different order from those described in the first three parts of the novel. "Epilogue" is devoted solely to Gilles's experience of the Spanish Civil War, first as a fascist agent under the pseudonym of Paul Walter and later as a French journalist covering the fighting in Extremadura. On both occasions he chooses to involve himself actively in the struggle and the book leaves him in a desperate situation from which he is unlikely to emerge alive. The style, atmosphere, and perspective embraced in "Epilogue" form a stark contrast to the immobility and the sense of imminent social collapse that characterize the preceding section. All Gilles's senses come alive and the transformation that he observes in himself and in his environment confirms the judgment that he had passed on the state of the society he had left: "Everything had changed: the world and he too [. . .] He was totally 'in the realm of facts,' as teachers, away in their quiet schools, put it" (448–49).

The views of the Civil War that Gilles presents come from the geographical peripheries of Spain (the Balearic Islands and the extreme western side of the country) and the encounters in which he is involved take place away from the main centers of fighting. They are described, moreover, by one who, despite his involvement, remains essentially an outsider. These two facts enable Gilles to maintain a relative objectivity in his description and lead him to make constant comparisons between this country and the whole European situation with which he, as a journalist, is familiar. By this means the Civil War is presented as a consequence of the social situation described earlier in the novel and also as the forerunner to a Europe-wide conflagration. Gazing at some simple strong peasants fighting for the Phalangists, Gilles describes them as "that eternally primitive race that still fills the depths of Europe and from which is now emerging that great irresistible movement that is startling tender minds in the cities of the West" (493–94). His decision to take up arms and fight beside these peasants is a desperate effort to become part of this "great movement."

Although the description of political and social events of the interwar years constitutes a relatively firm historical setting for *Gilles* and provides a fascinating, if extremely biased, view of particular aspects of that era, most attention in the novel is focused on the progress of the central character as he seeks to understand himself and adapt to his society. When living with Pauline in Paris, Gilles, we are told, "was not at all thinking of writing to be read, but simply to fix each stage of his inner development" (372). The novel as a whole is most profitably viewed from a similar perspective. Despite their considerable intrinsic interest, the events in which Gilles is involved take on their full significance only insofar as they affect him personally. The very structure of the work indicates this, the four parts of the novel corresponding to the four distinct stages in Gilles's development.

Since Gilles never really adapts to postwar society, "La Permission" might be considered an appropriate title to cover the whole period he spends in Paris prior to his return to action in Spain. In the novel, however, it refers specifically to the period when the memories of war are still sufficiently vivid to make impossible any sustained effort to adapt and to create a coherent social self. Commitment is not in question for the young soldier attracted both to action and to ease, and this inability to choose is reflected in the constant questioning to which he subjects himself. Alone in Myriam's room and surrounded by her wealth—but significantly still in uniform—he sees reflected in her mirror the uncertainty of his psychological state: "The soldier's features had detached themselves like a mask; underneath, the features of the austere student that he had been were not to be found either" (53). The state of psychological limbo suggested by this mirror reflection is expressed from time to time by Drieu in words that in some respects recall the terminology being developed almost contemporaneously by Sartre in *La Nausée* [Nausea] and *L'Etre et le néant* [Being and Nothingness]. Gilles sees himself as "the chance instrument that destiny had grasped" (154) and feels that he is floating like "a ghost that is perniciously light, fallaciously transparent" (50) around other beings whose opacity and density he envies.

Gilles gradually becomes conscious of the fact that an image of his self over which he has no control is being formed and projected on to him by others. He senses that this image, for which he is nevertheless largely responsible, threatens to bind him into a situation that he cannot accept. Such a situation has developed in particular with Myriam, and he reacts with despair: "Never again would he manage to break free of the image of himself which had gradually taken shape outside of him as a result of semisincerity, semihypocrisy, absent-mindedness, humor, and which he saw reflected in Myriam's eyes" (98).

It is principally to escape such an unacceptable definition of the self and to discover and manifest a self that has greater authenticity that Gilles first visits Carentan, and then later volunteers for active military service. Of unknown parentage, Gilles has been brought up by Carentan and senses that his education by the old man, like the experience of war, has imprinted itself indelibly on his personality. Back in the rugged natural environment of his early years, he recognizes the presence of "the soul of his childhood" (100), and the desire he expresses to Carentan to "ascertain the proportion of myself that still remains from you" (111) indicates that for him this "soul" continues to exist in some measure within his person. The decision to return to front line fighting so soon after his marriage is, of course, a rather more desperate effort at self-definition. His inability to relate sexually to Myriam has left him with an intolerable conviction of his "carnal lie," his "moral crime," and his "physical defilement" (144). The return to the front is a quest for purification from such sins and illustrates his continued faith in the possibility of authentic self-discovery. At Belfort, where he is stationed, "he was aware that he was different from the way he had been in Paris" (154). Some years later he describes this idealized self as "open, lost in a world of faith, infinitely vulnerable, incapable of cleverness and prudence, to be taken like a gift, broken like a hope" (204).

During his visit to Carentan in Normandy Gilles had expressed his unwillingness to adopt the customary way of life of his mentor and had exclaimed in a tone of distress: "It is imperative that I come to terms with my age" (113). This is the necessity with which Gilles lives in the pages of "L'Elysée" as he seeks to define himself in relation to the social realities of the day. The change in emphasis from "La Permission" is indicated in the very first pages where Gilles's point of view, previously dominant, is quite absent. His name is raised only in passing, and he appears as just one member among others of a particular social group. In the five or so years since the war, Gilles has apparently become absorbed into the social and political world to which his marriage to Myriam has provided access. It is clear, however, that such assimilation has been at the price of the integrity of his "fundamental self" which continues to assert itself: the conflict that had expressed itself with such violent naiveté in "La Permission" continues to simmer. Its presence is not only discerned by the more perceptive of his friends, who, like Dora, at times, wonder precisely who he is; it is also attested by Gilles's own self-condemnation. In a revealing statement which indicates his awareness of the extent to which he has assimilated to society, he complains to Dora: "I am not the person I wanted you to love" (281).

"L'Elysée" contains several incidents that serve to penetrate the newly developed social sophistication of Gilles and recall the ideal, natural self that social intercourse has obscured. The most noteworthy is the short visit that he and Dora make to the forest of Lyons. In a passage that shows Drieu's Romanticism at its most extreme and suggests his debt to Rousseau, Gilles relates his true self to the noble majesty of the tall trees and allows his imagination to conceive a new more satisfying future with his mistress: "With her he would leave Paris, once again he would take up the straight thread of his instinct, he would plunge back into the depths of nature, into complete silence, he would open himself to the voice of the universe" (214). Such resolutions are, however, shortlived and tend to fade in the stifling atmosphere of the capital. Significantly, the personal crisis that his break with Dora represents for him is later conveyed by the image of an uprooted forest giant.

Viewed in terms of Gilles's efforts to relate satisfactorily to his age, "L'Elysée" is a tale of almost unmitigated failure. Every step in the direction of social assimilation is construed as a betrayal, and only away from the modern city is the authentic self able to appear. This is the attitude that Gilles chooses to adopt as he extends his experience of postwar Paris society. It is an attitude that provokes in him an increasingly extreme psychological change in the remaining two sections of the novel.

"L'Apocalypse," with the connotations that the title carries of finality and destruction, opens with Gilles's resignation from his post in the Ministry of Foreign Affairs and his retreat to the deserts of Algeria. Both these actions indicate a desperate, if naive, attempt to cut all ties with a society whose influence has produced in him a personality as divided as his body, which is described here for the first time: "This body was disconcerting: it was in two parts like an anatomy model. On one side, it was the body of a fully developed and almost athletic man, with a broad solid neck, square full shoulder, well formed breast, narrow hip, well set knee; on the other side it was a carcass that was blasted, tortured, twisted, withered, puny" (363–64). In the "plenitude" that the solitude of the desert paradoxically brings, he dreams of a society in which man is allowed the freedom to contemplate, to pray, and hence to live out the full possibilities of his being: "Here solitude is man with his wealth, with his sky, with his earth, with his soul, with the harshness of the only wealth he has, with hunger, with thirst, with the lost cry of prayer" (365). Finally, however, the trip to Algeria and the break with Parisian society assume their inevitable reality as a Romantic interlude without the possibility of continuance. Gilles seeks to prolong the experience by living with the unsophisticated Pauline, met in Algiers, and by striving to maintain financial and intellectual independence by producing his own journal, "L'Apocalypse." Social forces, however, prove too strong and he ends his Parisian life sunk deeper than ever in the way of living he abhors.

The experiences of "L'Apocalypse," disillusioning as they ultimately are, nevertheless provide Gilles with confirmation of the truth briefly glimpsed at the end of "L'Elysée": man finds himself only by projecting himself out of the narrow confines of his individuality. Reflecting on the importance of friendship, Gilles describes a friend as "a unique opportunity to know something about the world other than oneself" (384) and his relationship with Pauline is valued for similar reasons. She enables him to tear his life from its "egotistical center" (410) and reveal the "prodigious possibilities" (411) that lie buried in its depths. The symbol of such outgoing is the child that Pauline conceives. With the child aborted, Pauline dead, and the "Apocalypse" experiment a dismal failure, Gilles is free for a last desperate effort to find the elusive self that normal social contact obscures. The direction of this effort is indicated by his reflection: "Were not the only places where he had been himself those places where he had managed to be merely a brief brilliant prayer, a lost cry, on the battlefields or in the desert?" (440). Self-discovery is to be achieved through suppression of the socially determined individual.

This strict dichotomy between the "authentic self" and the "social individual" is central to "Epilogue." Walter claims that "his interest in other individuals had died with his interest in his own individuality" (471) and his whole activity in Spain may be seen as an attempt to translate this loss of interest into a complete suppression of what he considers to be its pernicious expressions in his own life. Walter (and Gilles) see the reaction of fear as the principal assertion by the individual of his particularity, and it is against this that their efforts are specially directed. Forced to flee for his life with a young fellow Fascist, Walter dreams of taking a stand: "Flee, once again flee, keep on fleeing. Enough. Do something else than flee. Fight" (474). This in fact is what he is finally enabled to do when, as Gilles the French journalist, he overcomes the temptations to evacuate the Plaza de Toros under attack from the Republicans, commits himself to the Fascist cause, and takes up a rifle. Through this action, in which the individual with his fears for personal safety melts into the exaltation of collective endeavor, Gilles succeeds in "finding himself" (500). Moreover, the surroundings in which he chooses to die give his act particular symbolic value. Since the Plaza de Toros is "modern and ugly" (494), symbolizing all that he detests about the society of his time, he appears as a latter-day Samson, a role which Carentan had previously suggested as appropriate for him. He dies amidst the destruction of the society by which he has been misled through the agency of woman. His protest has, however, been made and his authentic self affirmed.

As both this view of Gilles's death and the mythicoreligious terms of the last page suggest, the whole incident in Extremadura takes on the most general significance. For Gilles himself this general significance is expressed most clearly in the belief that action and thought have finally been linked. Now he is *living* an idea, and the conjunction of what have proved to be irreconcilable in his experience of society brings a new richness to his life: "Each day he was giving more of his life to this idea and it was giving it back to him a hundredfold. In the world, he was probably one of those spirits who were giving to this idea the breath essential to its life" (493). In this way his role in life is finally formulated. With humility which, despite his exultation, he considers appropriate, Gilles concludes: "I am one of those humble souls who help action and thought constantly to renew their compromised union" (496). Ironically, such a role is found to be possible only outside the framework of normal social living.

One of the fascinating structural features of the novel is the role played by the various women in Gilles's life. Each of the first three parts is dominated by a particular liaison which reflects closely Gilles's aspirations and state of mind at that period and enables him to see himself with greater clarity. There are, moreover, a number of other women who, though only briefly mentioned, reflect important aspects of Gilles's personality.

Marriage to Myriam Falkenberg is never considered by Gilles as other than a means of access to the glittering world of luxury that so attracts him on the first night of his leave. Myriam is in fact so identified by Gilles with this world that he has difficulty in distinguishing her physical characteristics: "And the things that she represented, that she offered him were so numerous and so desirable that he forgot her body" (38). Moreover, in a statement that probably indicates acceptance of the inevitable, even Carentan counsels marriage with Myriam as an instrument of social adaptation and self-understanding. He offers this advice to his protégé: "Well, get married, you'll learn from it. It's a quick, profound opportunity to learn what is your real relationship with the modern world" (112). Carentan too sees Myriam not in personal terms but as an aspect of the world to which Gilles desires to relate.

The idealized Alice figure, who appears in the latter pages of "La Permission" shortly after the marriage, serves as a structural counter-balance to the baser side of Gille's personality portrayed through Myriam. Still serving men in the theater of war as a nurse, Alice combines "strength that is fully developed and fully given" (148–49) with the "humble acceptance of a mother" (160) and recalls to Gilles the "moral virtues" (162) which his experience in Paris has led him to abandon but which remain to haunt his conscience. In particular she has little money, and has no need of wealth to satisfy her few needs. Alice represents all those aspects of Gilles's authentic self whose suppression makes a satisfactory relationship with Myriam impossible.

Several other women in "La Permission" serve to mediate the conflict in Gilles's soul. Despite his shocked reaction to the romantic overtures of his wartime nurse, Mabel Highland, Gilles has a brief affair with her but then leaves her suddenly, apparently dimly aware that she reflects his own moral decline from the harsh purity of war to the ease of urban living. The woman known simply as l'Autrichienne is also evoked at crucial moments in the relationship with Myriam. Her introduction has an effect similar to that of Gilles's periodic visits to the brothel: she represents a possibly only partly conscious assertion by Gilles of his authentic self hidden behind the facade which he presents to Myriam and which she chooses to accept. "You are always blackening yourself" (99), she complains when, in a moment of remorse, Gilles tries to indicate the true nature of his attraction to her. She summarily dismisses all his halfhearted attempts at confession and Gilles is obliged to seek such other ways as lie to hand to express the reality of the life he is living. Gilles's visits to the brothel are, moreover, seen as a positive affirmation from another point of view: they symbolize rejection of the social respectability that at bottom he abhors.

In "L'Elysée" Gilles's personal life—and to a large extent his attitude to society—is dominated by his liaison with the American Dora Reading. At a time when assimilation to bourgeois society is causing him to lose touch with the realities he had briefly experienced during the war and in the arms of Alice, Dora comes to confirm his faith in life and his sense of personal authenticity. Like Alice a combination of "athlete" and "mother" (195), she unites in her body the virtues of earth and heaven as she assumes in his mind no less than cosmic dimensions: "Long legs, long hips; long hips on long legs. A powerful thorax, dancing on a supple waist. Higher up, in the clouds, square, broad shoulders, a shining bar. Higher still, beyond the clouds, the solar profusion of her blond hair" (194). In her Gilles discovers the "thicknesses" (263) that make her his point of contact with life and hence enable him to feel a unified personality. In a moment of exaltation he cries: "That's who that woman is, she's me, she's me finally encountered, recognized, greeted. Joy. The joy of finally being at ease with myself" (195). On her depends not only his faith in life but also his coherence as a person.

"L'Elysée" traces the progressive collapse of this rapturous vision, a process which is closely paralleled by Gilles's growing distress at the political and social life of Paris. Dora, whom certain, apparently chance, remarks indicate to be quite a normal imperfect individual, takes fright at the unreality of Gilles's vision, senses the dangerously insecure realms into which he would lead her, and finally repairs to the dull certainties of her diplomat husband. The effect on Gilles is predictable: the world loses its reality and his personality becomes double, "cracked" into two parts that resume their prior function of commenting on the thoughts and actions of the other. "He looked at himself in the mirror and heard himself saying in an undertone things that were trivial and cynical" (277).

The extravagance of Gilles's vision of Dora is in itself sufficient indication that she is largely a projection of his own desires. The collapse of the liaison is not so much the result of a change of heart on her part as an inevitable conflict between his romantic imaginings and the claims of reality. On numerous occasions Dora pleads with Gilles to recognize that she is not the woman he believes her to be, but he is as unprepared to listen to her as Myriam had been unwilling to accept his attempted confessions. The Dora imagined by Gilles is quite simply an expression of a psychological necessity. Early in the liaison Gilles watches Dora dancing and muses: "Was that skin an illusion? He was passionately anxious that it should be a total reality, that this woman should be there in her fullness. Thus his jealousy was on the one hand a feeling related to nature and animality, and on the other hand the anxious vibration of his desire for moral plenitude" (197). He allows himself to imagine her as an idealized synthesis of the antithetical figures of Myriam and Alice. She has the moral and physical qualities of the one with the social situation and money of the other. In the final analysis she represents a desperate effort by Gilles to find in society and through woman the values that he wishes to maintain. His liaison with her consequently may be seen as the story of a personal ideal seeking to survive in a hostile environment but failing. The parallels with Gilles's incursions into the political world are obvious.

Even more clearly than Alice, Pauline, who accompanies Gilles as mistress and then as wife through the period of "L'Apocalypse," reflects Gilles's continuing ideal and the changed nature of his social attitudes. Encountered on the other side of the Mediterranean following Gilles's exhilarating experiences of the solitude of the desert, Pauline welcomes the relative privation in which Gilles chooses to live now that he has broken social ties. Her total self-giving, expressed notably in her rejection of financial security offered by a rich lover, arouses in Gilles a renewed sense of the energies of the self that have long lain dormant. Like Dora, she provides a focus for the self-abnegation that paradoxically brings self-fulfillment: "His life was irresistibly wrenched from its egotistical center, his life no longer gravitated around his self, but was setting off in a powerful new direction toward an unknown destination. He was finding that he had enormous capacities for unselfishness, prodigious possibilities for growth" (410).

In the final pages of "L'Apocalypse" Gilles's private life and his attitude to society leave the parallel paths that they have followed up to this point to unite in an image of Pauline that identifies her with the fate of the nation. Now sophisticated, diseased, and sterile, she does not merely reflect, but in a sense *becomes,* the society from which Gilles is finally to turn in despair. She dies, significantly, in the days between the two Stavisky demonstrations, the political divisions of the nation being symbolized by the collapse prior to death of her senses of sight and hearing. Like her, the Left and the Right are blind and deaf to each other and this situation threatens to destroy the living fabric of society. Moreover, in a clear reference to what he sees as one of the basic social problems of his age—a problem he later explores in *Notes pour comprendre le siècle*—Drieu notes in his description of Pauline that "the channels between her soul and her body were already cut" (439). Indeed, so associated are Pauline and France in Gilles's mind at this moment that he expresses the shortcomings in his conduct toward them both in similar terms: "[. . .] it was too late to remedy the failure of his love for Pauline. And it was long before February 6 that he should have helped France. France was dying while Pauline was dying" (440). His betrayal of Pauline in taking as his mistress the pitiful Berthe Santon has been no less culpable than his lack of commitment to his country in its time of need.

Insofar as they are an important vehicle for the presentation of Gilles's social attitudes, the women in the novel provide a link between the personal and the social. As such they focus attention on Drieu's abiding problem of the validity of a particular individual's vision of society. Does one's private life determine the view that one takes of the state of society or does it simply reflect society? To what extent can one isolate the functions of the biographer, in particular the autobiographer, from those of social critic? Is Montaigne's dictum "know thyself" impossible of application? If so, of what social significance and value is the work of the writer who reflects upon the self and presents its vision of reality? These are some of the questions that Drieu poses either directly or by implication in the pages of *Gilles*. They serve to bring into uneasy synthesis the two principal emphases of his writing in the interwar period and indicate an increased awareness of the theoretical problems of his craft. From this point of view *Gilles* is an interesting attempt to fulfill, in fictional form, the criteria for validity laid down some years previously in *Genève ou Moscou* [Geneva or Moscow]: "The judgments of a man of letters on the whole of society can be accepted only if they are accompanied by a pitiless analysis of the individual conditions that determine them."[5]

Gilles himself is aware of the likelihood of projecting personal problems and obsessions onto one's view of society and into one's political beliefs. In his dealings with politicians and their parties he tends to disregard doctrines and labels and to seek the psychological reality of the individual who presents them: "[. . .] he knew that behind the motives that are termed 'selfish' there are always psychological determinants which are much more decisive" (403). He is doubly conscious in himself of this danger of projection, especially in the latter stages of his life in Paris when his vision of society grows steadily darker. He is prepared to recognize a certain voluptuous attraction in his nature toward the idea of decadence (401), he is suspicious of the disgust that comes so easily to him when he contemplates the political life of the Third Republic, and in consequence he frequently seeks external confirmation of his inner convictions.

Authorial comment and the point of view of other characters also indicate Drieu's awareness of the problems raised by the mingling of the social and the personal. At the same time it is clear that he is conscious of the difficulty of treating each in isolation. On numerous occasions attempts are made to situate Gilles in other than his own terms. From time to time he is removed from center stage and attention is given to the view that others have of him and his obsessions. For example, Gilles's interest is aroused by a friend's description of his attraction to war as an attempt to construct a "philosophy of life on resistance to diarrhoea" (88). Dora Reading reflects at length on Gilles's personality and ideas, and the comparison she makes between him and her husband serves to reveal the extent to which Gilles is at odds with modern society. Perhaps the clearest attempt to place Gilles's psychology into a sociological framework—and certainly one of the most telling commentaries on the enigmas of his personality—may be found in the last pages of "L'Elysée" in a conversation about Gilles between a priest and a

Catholic writer:

> "[. . .] he's a man from our Western provinces lost in your terrible Paris."
> "Oh no, father," exclaimed a Catholic writer, "he's the most perverse kind of Parisian."
> "One does not exclude the other." (441)

In the 1942 preface to *Gilles* Drieu treats these problems of personal vision and external reality from the particular perspective of the imaginative writer. As the individual's particular views cannot fail to be influenced by the prevailing social ethos, so the writer's necessarily personal vision of society must be expressed in forms that are largely socially determined. Since "no author, not even one whose work is supremely lacking in realism can escape his memory" (8) the writer inevitably reflects himself in his work, even when he appears to be at his most objective. On the other hand the very process of expression necessarily involves a certain distortion of reality: "The economy of the literary work, the necessities of composition and presentation produce as much falsification as what people are in the habit of calling invention and which is simply the conformity of the author with himself, with the law of his inner world" (8). This Drieu finds as true of the writer's description of himself as of his presentation of the outside world. In this way he refutes the rather simplistic approach of those who would see in the characters of much of his fiction a barely modified transposition of his own life.

In this preface, however, Drieu carries his treatment of the issue rather further than the exploratory stage of the text of *Gilles.* He appears to accept the limitations imposed by literary creation and to become convinced of the value of his vision within these limits. He uses the idea of "refraction" to describe the process of distortion by which both inner vision and external reality receive expression in the literary work. The latter, however, remains for him a document of considerable significance from the very fact that it is an historic individual's response to a specific social situation and as such a valid expression of life at one point in time: "But changing the facts is not changing the spirit of the facts and Balzac is just like Michelet, that man of such extraordinary imagination, in giving supreme service to what alone counts, life. If one creates life one does not lie, one does not deceive, for life always echoes life precisely" (9).

The text of *Gilles* may thus be seen to lead to this important theoretical statement of the writer's function, in which Drieu seeks to come to terms with the demands of his creative imagination. Accepting a certain distortion of reality as inevitable, he nevertheless proclaims belief in the ultimate value of the work produced, the degree of "refraction" imposed by the conditions of creation being considered as socially significant in itself. From this point of view the question of the validity or the representative nature of a writer's work barely arises. He is free to pursue his art in the knowledge that, however personal its form may make it seem, it remains a valid reflection of an aspect of the society in which he creates.

It is significant that from this point in time Drieu tends to produce works in whose conception the element of individual imagination is more dominant than previously. As the remarks on Balzac and Michelet suggest, his approach to literary creation has widened, and he tends to see his activity in a perspective broader than that of his own narrow social situation. This breadth of perspective is seen very clearly in his subsequent novel *L'Homme à cheval*.

Chapter Six

Art, Sacrifice, and the Cosmic Order

L'Homme à cheval

Pierre-Henri Simon considered *L'Homme à cheval* [The Man on Horseback] to be Drieu's major achievement in the field of the novel,[1] and most readers of Drieu rate it highly. Written some four years after *Gilles,* it was published during the Occupation in 1943 and indicates a profound change in Drieu's imaginative writing. Now that the Gille figure has "found himself" in action and death in the Spanish Civil War, there emerges a new fictional figure who, although caught up to some degree in the social and political affairs of his age, has his principal interests elsewhere. The first example of this new figure, who is to reappear in various guises in Drieu's three wartime novels, is Felipe the guitarist.

Felipe recounts the rise to power and the subsequent actions of Jaime Torrijos, a lieutenant in a Bolivian cavalry regiment, who succeeds, with Felipe's help, in overthrowing the aging dictator don Benito Ramirez. Once in a position of supreme power, Jaime, the man on horseback, pursues his goal of humbling the wealthy Spanish classes and securing the support of the Indian and half-caste majority, in whom he believes the country's hopes lie. With this power base he plans to present a united front to the surrounding countries and to force access for Bolivia to the sea. These social and political plans collapse, however, when the forces of the Establishment, represented by the Jesuit Florida, and the Mason Belmez, provoke the Indian population to revolt. Jaime is obliged to use harsh repressive measures to restore order and his subsequent war against Chile and Peru is lost. These setbacks cause him to give up his wider ambitions of creating a federation of Bolivia, Chile, and Peru and of achieving full emancipation for the Indians. He finally abandons his position of Protector, symbolically sacrifices his horse at Lake Titicaca, and disappears into the Amazon jungles.

Structurally, *L'Homme à cheval* is in many respects similar to *Gilles.* Each novel has four parts and each part recounts a similar stage in the development of the figure that gives the novel its title. The first part of *L'Homme à cheval,* entitled "Le Cigare de Don Benito" [Don Benito's Cigar], relates the entry of a young soldier into the social and political life of his country. As in *Gilles,* access to this world is achieved largely by the death of an aging disillusioned father figure. In the second part, which takes its title from the beautiful but perfidious aristocrat Doña Camilla Bustamente, there is an unwilling but perceptible assimilation of Jaime to the refinement of the aristocrats with whom he has to deal. This assimilation, which Jaime fears and against which he rebels at one stage in rather spectacular fashion, is largely brought about through a woman. As in *Gilles,* this woman, despite her social ties and assimilating effect, is able to bring to Jaime profound knowledge of himself. The tension of Gille's relationship with Dora is mirrored on the one hand by Jaime's admission to Camilla that it was thanks to her that "he was coming to know himself, that he was finding himself" (110) and on the other hand by Felipe's observation that Jaime is beginning to resemble Don Benito. The third part, "La Révolte des Indiens" [The Revolt of the Indians], tells of the failure of Jaime's plans for his country and his apparent renunciation of any further significant political initiative. Like Gilles at the time of Pauline's death, Jaime believes the forces of desirable progress in his country to be dead. The resemblances between "Epilogue" and the fourth part of *L'Homme à cheval,* "Le Lac Titicaca" [Lake Titicaca], are quite obvious. In both there is not only a renunciation of social and political action within one's society but also a retreat or escape from society itself. It is significant that it should be on a note of sacrifice that both novels end.

Despite these striking similarities of structure between *Gilles* and *L'Homme à cheval,* there are considerable differences of point of view and tone. The tale of Jaime Torrijos is recounted in the first person by one who is essentially a spectator of the action, even though it is he who frequently prompts this action at crucial stages in Jaime's career. Felipe's customary situation during periods of action is suggested quite early in the novel. Captured by Don Benito's men, he is obliged to witness from the height of a tower the abortive initial attack by Jaime and his cavalry. In such a vantage point he feels himself a traitor to his friends but is unable to take any part in the action, even though later the knowledge he gains enables Jaime to make a successful counterattack. Felipe's separation from the mainstream of action is indicated by numerous other images during the course of the novel. Almost invariably he is found riding a recalcitrant mule rather than a horse, the novel's symbol of action. Furthermore, one suspects that his constant stress on his gross ugliness is a reflection of his inability to enter the aesthetically attractive world of action. Consequently Felipe appears in the novel as essentially a man of ideas. Through the words and music of his songs, he suggests most of Jaime's major undertakings, but, despite himself, he remains an observer, separated from the realities of action in the world. Such distance is, moreover, indicated in the novel's epigraph with its suggestion of a voice crying in the wilderness: "Woe to him who would keep silent in the middle of the desert believing that his voice was heard by no one" (5). The sense of isolation in this first image is reflected at the very end of the novel as Jaime moves off and leaves Felipe bereft.

Since, except for the postface, the story is told entirely from Felipe's point of view, there is only rarely a sense of close involvement with what is being described. The impression of distance and at times even detachment is such as to lead Frédéric Grover to remark that the characters "move in a rarefied atmosphere."[2] This sense of distance and detachment conveyed by Felipe's point of view is reinforced by various other literary devices. The story is situated, for example, not only in a country geographically remote from Europe but also in a period which, though carefully specified, is relatively remote from the present. The most significant attempt by the author at *distanciation,* however, is found in the brief "postface" attributed to a narrator where even those geographical and historical facts on which the story depends for its impression of veracity are questioned and finally discounted. The text of the novel is revealed as coming from the writings of a certain Felipe, a strange old friend of the narrator's grandfather, who suspected that his friend was not a South American at all but a political refugee from Spain and, what is more, a "practical joker." The narrator confirms these suspicions by revealing that Jaime Torrijos never existed as an historical figure, that the story is seriously inaccurate in many respects and that it "seems to have been written by someone who never set foot in Bolivia, who at the very most dreamed about it" (254). In just a few lines the illusion of historicity is, through the introduction of the narrator, brutally destroyed and the story of Jaime Torrijos is removed to the status of the insubstantial dreaming of an imaginative nobody.

As in *Rêveuse bourgeoisie* following Geneviève's identification of herself as narrator, this revelation provokes a substantial reappraisal of the preceding pages. From the novel's fictional world Felipe emerges as the only character with "historical" reality, while Jaime becomes a creation of Felipe in an even more radical way than that indicated in the text. Jaime the Protector is a creation of Felipe not only in the sense that he provides the impulse to action. The very conception of the figure of Jaime is seen to be a product of the imagination of his "follower," a projection of his aspirations and ideals. In this way the novel becomes rather more complex than the obvious analysis it presents of the interaction of a man of thought and a man of action. By focusing on the dream of Felipe the artist and by specifying it as a construction of the guitarist's imagination, Drieu suggests that he is moving away from exclusive preoccupation with the individual's reaction to his particular historical situation. His interest is now centered on the nature of the artist's activity in the world, on the nature of the dreaming that produces the work of art. *L'Homme à cheval* is consequently an attempt to probe the recesses of the artistic imagination, to determine the relationship between the artistic imagination and life, and to understand the processes by which the artistic self projects itself in literary creation.

The element water in its tranquil feminine mode is used at the beginning of the novel to indicate the nature of Felipe's dream before the entry of Jaime into his life. Felipe speaks of his dream as an undisturbed pool of water, an image consonant with the detachment from the world induced by his theological studies. This image of water unruffled by the action of men and evocative of the divine recurs also at the end of the novel in the form of Lake Titicaca, which is described as "a great eye contemplating the heavens" (251). Significantly it is here that Jaime performs his sacrificial renunciation of action before passing from Felipe's life.

Felipe introduces Jaime into his life to disturb this natural tranquillity. For reasons that he does not fully understand, artistic creation through his guitar and the mysteries of theology do not satisfy him and the need for action asserts itself. "[. . .] I desired to introduce perilous figures into the intimate circle of myself" (10) he confesses, and it is for this reason that Jaime gains entry to his life. In an image rich in symbolism Jaime is described by Felipe as "a stone that I was casting into the water of my dream" (28). The male harshness of stone comes to disturb the fragile feminine surface of the water. In so doing it creates the ripples that temporarily obscure the unity of earth and heaven that the reflection of the water eternally proclaims. The ripples are the events of Felipe's life during his twenty years as "follower" of Jaime, before the stone finally disappears from sight and the ripples subside. In his conversation with Felipe at Lake Titicaca Jaime uses similar imagery when he confesses that in his social and political action he has been unable to "conquer Lake Titicaca" (238). Such a concept of conquest remains largely undefined, but for Jaime it at least involves some control over the "ripples of action" that he causes.

Action consequently emerges as an inner need for Felipe and the desired dynamism in his life is projected on and communicated by the figure of Jaime. Initially Jaime is presented as a creature of unreflective action, as a "beautiful blind plant" (19) developing toward "the sun of its destiny with admirable lack of consciousness" (19). He is totally the creation of his guitarist companion, who directs his action, teaches him who he is and values him as his "point of fecundation" (77). Gradually, however, Felipe loses control of his marionette and becomes increasingly astonished at Jaime's developing powers of thought. Like Gide in *Les Faux-monnayeurs* [The Counterfeiters] wondering what his characters will do next, Felipe describes himself as "a god whose creation is progressively slipping from his control" (191). The entry of the dynamic realities of life into the realms of the dream produces unforeseen ramifications. Felipe muses: "Thought, once it has become action, tempered with blood, forged like a weapon of steel, is foreign to the thinker" (198).

Jaime Torrijos is not simply a projection of Felipe's need of strength and action. He is also, and perhaps principally, a means of realizing Felipe's aestheic aspirations. At Lake Titicaca Felipe presents Jaime as the idealized form of his dream and adds: "I, as a lover of beauty, rushed toward that form, which was beauty incarnate" (236). The beauty of such strength in action is given perhaps its most spectacular expression in Felipe's ecstatic description of the abortive charge by Jaime and his men against Don Benito. In language that recalls in some measure the charge at Charleroi, Felipe, gazing from his tower of captivity, exclaims:

O magnificent array of animal breasts advancing toward us, coming up toward us! O manes! O tails! O foam! O long cry now lost! The mystery of humanity offering itself up for nothing, to nothing! Oh beauty frenetically self-sufficient! O minute forever lost, forever eternal in the heart! (52–53)

Felipe's interest lies totally in the aesthetics of action, in beauty in motion, and all his efforts are directed to the creation of situations that will allow such beauty to manifest itself. Immediately before Jaime's successful counterattack, he becomes aware that the goal of the operation has ceased to occupy his attention. Later he notes with some surprise that he had "invented" not only the Protector that Jaime has become but also the Protector's enemies, so that aesthetically pleasing conflict would ensue.

The latter examples show that ideological or even partisan considerations count for little in Felipe's eyes. Though he encourages Jaime to depose Don Benito, he remains open to the charm of the latter's strong male voice and recognizes that had he met Don Benito before Jaime he might well be on the other side. He is in fact quite cynical about political change, believing that "no system has ever existed except the free-for-all" (31). In the present situation, however, he recognizes that Don Benito's strength is failing, that he is, in the words of Jaime's mistress, "ugly" and must be swept aside by the stronger forces of life. The cigar, perpetually in his lips and the "final symbol of his consciousness" (63), falls to the floor of the convent chapel and is replaced by the more forcefully masculine dagger which plunges into his heart.

Felipe's tendency to give his political allegiance to those forces most likely to manifest the energy and beauty of life lead him to oppose the aristocracy and the bourgeoisie represented by Florida and Belmez. Both these groups have for Felipe lost contact with life, are incapable of creativity, and spend their time, like Florida, spoiling "life's rare expressions of beauty" (105). The aristocrats are, in Jaime's words, "headless men walking about out of habit" (197). Their distance from the creative energies of life and the consequent precariousness of their situation are symbolized by the position of Camilla Bustamente's apartment. It is built out over the deep valleys where the Indians live close to the soil. When the forces of nature grow violent she takes refuge in safer, more substantial quarters. Florida's retreat is similarly situated and enables him to remain "quite free of links with the earth" (192) cultivating the flowers that, like the aristocrats, are destined soon to wither. Jaime and his creator, however, strive to keep contact with what are considered the more basic realities of life. Jaime proclaims to the assembled grandees in his palace that all strength and beauty lie in the people with their earthy roughness, and he illustrates this romantic belief through a spectacular exhibition of dancing by his mistress Conchita. Felipe expresses this physical and emotional need for contact with the earth by paying periodic visits to the Indian tribes in which he finds "the images of [his] most secret desires" (87). Bound to the earth and its spirits, and subsisting grimly among the filth and vermin that is their lot, these Indian tribes, through their life and art, display strength and beauty that are not found in the comfortable halls of the wealthy.

Felipe's experience of political commitment to the lower classes and to Jaime gradually brings him to an awareness of the nature of the political facet of his dream. Since ideological considerations and self-interest count for little, he comes to understand that politics is for him an exalted concept, related to his intellectual, spiritual, and emotional expectations of life. Encouragement of union between Jaime and Camilla, for example, is for him much more than the clever political strategy that it is for Florida: "But between Jaime and Camilla there was something more profound than politics, or rather there was politics of such rare profundity as to reveal its links with poetry, music and, who knows, perhaps high religion" (105). It is Felipe's dream that the political, with its possibilities of action in the world, should be linked with the aesthetic and spiritual facets of life. Such a dream explains his statement that the couple Jaime-Camilla constituted his whole universe.

Felipe's idealized concept of politics draws attention to the quest for unity that underlies every aspect of his dream. As the principal focus for this dream, Jaime becomes a clearly representative figure. Unity and unification mark the political program that he proposes, and, as a Spanish-Indian half-caste, he unites in his person the two ethnic elements of his country's population. Jaime is "politics in its entirety" (166). Strength and beauty unite to characterize his action in the world and it is through him that Felipe learns not only that thought and action can achieve a point of juncture but that each withers in isolation. In one of the last reported conversations before the retirement to Lake Titicaca, Felipe, in a moment of exaltation, expresses to Camilla his vision of the unity that Jaime enshrines: "Jaime is a unity, from which nothing can be separated without bringing the death of the whole.

Jaime is the body of a horseman, the soul of a hermit and the spirit of a captain. [. . .] Jaime is all or nothing. Jaime is Bolivia" (212). Elsewhere this unity is expressed in rather more extravagant imagery. Jaime is described as "the perfect androgyne" (213) and also, in a reference to the unity of thought and action, as "a centaur, a leader of centaurs" (245). At one stage his figure even assumes cosmic dimensions as his steps are seen as related to the path of the stars overhead.

Felipe's dream of life's unity also receives expression through his vision of the geographical features of Bolivia. High mountains "with their burden of indestructible snows" (41) suggest the silence and immensity of the heavens, while the deep valleys provide men with the means to sustain life. But mountains and valleys form one country and teach that life is one. Felipe explains: "[. . .] when I speak of spirits of the earth, it is not to set them over against the spirits of the sky. For the sky is just as present as the earth, especially among us who are equally at home in one as in the other" (88). It is, however, in Lake Titicaca, a terrestrial element eternally reflecting the immensity and beauty of the heavens, that Felipe finds his most perfect expression of unity. In this place the sense of the divine imposes itself, but equally one has the impression of being in close contact with the earth: the divine and the terrestrial, sky and earth, are one. It is here, moreover, that Felipe becomes clearly conscious of the religious side of Jaime Torrijos and concludes that "a great soldier is always a great ascetic" (233). Situated at the junction of Peru and Bolivia, Lake Titicaca takes on political significance. Here the frontier between the two countries is not visible, and there are neither soldiers nor customs officers to show the foolish barriers that men erect between countries that belong together. In this lake Jaime and Felipe find the unity which existed in the time of the Incas and which Jaime has been unable to reestablish by political means. Gradually Lake Titicaca takes on wider symbolic significance. It does not merely symbolize the essential unity of two countries but of the whole continent. The lake, which for Felipe is limitless, "enshrines the whole of South America" (237) and constitutes by its very existence the realization in eternity of the political dream of Jaime and Felipe.

As Lake Titicaca manifests for eternity the ultimate unity of the universe, so does the sacrifice by Jaime of his horse beside the lake enshrine in a moment of eternity the values for which he has lived. It is hence significant that Lake Titicaca should give its name to the section of the novel in which this act is performed. Once again it is Felipe who breathes the idea of sacrifice into the man of action whom he has created, and it is he who proclaims its significance. In sacrifice the ultimate contradiction, that which opposes life to death, is resolved:

> Life and death came together in this host, this victim elevated by the priest. The eternal act of all religions, sacrifice, the act of sacrifice, which simply focuses and stylizes the act of living. Man is born only to die and he is never so much alive as when he is dying. But his life takes on meaning only if he gives his life instead of waiting for it to be taken from him. (242–43)

In this way Jaime's apparent act of renunciation assumes the force of strong affirmation. Through it the value of his life as a man of action is asserted, he forges a link with all previous generations of worshiping man and he proclaims the oneness of life and death. In sacrifice Felipe sees the mysteries of life that are evoked by the religious terminology of "fall, incarnation, redemption, holy sacrifice, Holy Spirit" (246) not only affirmed but unified into what he terms "a great metaphysical poem" (247).

In many respects *L'Homme à cheval* is one of Drieu's most personal works. Paradoxically, the abandonment of his century and his society leaves him free to express, through the character Felipe and without apology, his innermost ideals and aspirations. Criticism of contemporary twentieth-century European society is clearly not absent from this tale of nineteenth-century South America, but every element in the story serves to illuminate a particular vision of reality. The validity of such a vision is no longer a pressing question and the central affirmations in the work are proclaimed with the confidence of the prophet that the book's epigraph announces. *L'Homme à cheval* consequently marks a significant change in Drieu's continuing dialogue between the individual and society. Now the individual's vision occupies a place of undisputed dominance and the annoying trivialities of a society in decay are transcended by images of considerable power.

Through these undeniable personal elements in the novel, Drieu provides a more general reflection on the relationship between the artist's creative activity and the sources on which he draws, between the artistic imagination and life. In conversation at Lake Titicaca Felipe and Jaime both express their astonishment at the profound effect that each has had on the other. The suggestions conveyed by Felipe's guitar have transfigured the simple cavalry lieutenant from Agreda and this transformation has in its turn sharpened and enlarged the artist's vision. "I had brought action to Jaime, and without him my thought would have remained insignificant" (198). Felipe remains essentially a purveyor of words and he needs the reality of a Jaime to breathe into his words the richness of life and hence inspire his art. Jaime himself sees his mission as making words live and giving form to the dreams of others, while Felipe complements this with the statement that "each hero has the sustenance for ten great artists" (239).

At this level Felipe's dream becomes an affirmation of the interdependence of life and art. As Drieu remarked some months after the completion of the novel: "I have always been an artist, and I have become an even more complete one by taking a firm stance in other ways in my passionately held preferences."[3] Life with its disruptive, ultimately pointless, activity is received by the artist's imaginative faculties as an inner need and serves as a fertilizing and enriching influence. The expression of this influence by the artist in words and images further inspires the heroic man of action to probe life's possibilities, which are then celebrated in their beauty by the creative artist. This is the vision of art and life presented by Drieu through Felipe and Jaime. It constitutes a fascinating affirmation of the view he had of his role as a literary artist at a time when he saw his political commitment as headed for disaster.

Les Chiens de paille

In his April 1944 preface to *Les Chiens de paille* [The Straw Dogs] Drieu refers to the work as a "short fable" which he had written in the spring of the previous year in an attempt to give artistic form to "the most ephemeral, the most insidious current events" (9). He speaks specifically of two distinct levels of meaning in his fable, labeling them the "outer parts" or "exterior" and "the deeper substance" or "the living parts" (9). From the outset, therefore, Drieu invites the reader to look beyond the specific historical situation presented and to discern the more lasting elements in his creation, those that have been formed by his "artist's fingers" (10).

The "current events" that Drieu presents refer to the situation in France in 1942, just prior to the increased activity of the Resistance movement. The events take place in an unnamed coastal area in the northwest of the country. Constant Trubert, a fifty-year-old veteran of World War I, who has traveled widely outside France in the interwar years and who has recently escaped from a German prison camp, is sent to the area by Susini, his employer, who controls a black-market network. Constant occupies Susini's Maison des Marais and is told simply to familiarize himself with the region. He later learns that his real mission is to guard a store of arms and ammunition hidden in the cellar of the house after the 1940 defeat.

Constant's position as occupant of the Maison des Marais brings him into contact with representatives of the various political factions that have an interest in the store. He first meets Gabriel Salis, a Communist, who believes he has transcended narrow French patriotism in his politics and imagines himself closer to his Communist brothers in Russia than to his compatriots. Philippe Préault is the middle-class manager of a local metallurgy factory which is still in production. A Gaullist, his political sympathies go to the English, with whom he closely identifies. For Constant, Préault is a pathetic, rather repugnant figure, since he fails to understand that his identification with the English makes it impossible for him to preserve the distinctly French qualities that he claims to prize. Dr. Bardy, the third of those whom Susini terms "foreign agents" (56), relates to the Germans and is content to view the Occupation merely as a logical result of the 1940 defeat, for which he too had felt shame. In words that reflect much of Drieu's own thinking as expressed in his political essays and articles, Bardy proclaims himself a disabused nationalist, who between 1934 and 1936 had become aware that French nationalism needed external support. Forced to choose among England, Russia, and Germany, he had chosen the latter. He has now lost faith in German National-Socialism, and, while maintaining his commitment, awaits conquest by Russia with bitter satisfaction.

The most tragic figure in the conflict that develops is Jacques Cormont. At twenty-five, Cormont is younger than the others and remains staunchly idealistic. In his politics he strives to remain independent of foreign powers and hopes to revive the strength and vigor that he believes still exist in the French people. While he is unable to share Cormont's naive patriotism, Constant cannot remain unmoved, since he recognizes in the young man's enthusiasm the attitude that he himself had held in earlier years. With his badly scarred face, a legacy of his resistance to the German invasion several years before, Cormont is considered by Constant as a pitiable victim of French weakness. While the others are anxious that the arms and ammunition should remain in their present location for future use, Cormont leads a rash and ultimately abortive assault on the Maison des Marais and with Susini becomes a prisoner of Constant. Constant, totally disillusioned with the current political scene, lost in a mythicoreligious world and prepared for death, is about to blow up the house with all its occupants when bombs from a passing RAF plane destroy the house along with Préault's factory.

As a document of the war years, or as Drieu calls it "an irremediable document which bears the horrible palpitation of a moment" (10), the novel is of considerable interest. The complexities of the situation in France at that time are treated with a sympathy and an understanding that are perhaps surprising from one who, at least in his public life, continued to remain faithful to a Collaborationist point of view. It is true that Drieu is rather more severe on the Gaullist anglophile Préault than on the others, but this tends to be because of Préault's bourgeois attitudes and his hypocrisy rather than because of his political stance. The temporary but unlikely alliances that are made between Bardy and Cormont and between Salis and Préault serve as a reminder of the relativity of political ideology and the dangers of seeing the burning issues of the period in unduly simplistic terms. It is for reasons of this order that Frédéric Grover is led to speak of *Les Chiens de paille* as "a classic of Europe's agony."

Through the fascinating figure of Constant, with his aesthetic and religious preoccupations, this presentation of events in wartime France is transposed by Drieu to a more general level. Unwilling to tolerate the blind hopes and foolish pretensions of those who are politically committed, Constant expresses his desire for detachment from life's superficialities in two ways. He makes every effort to view contemporary history as a manifestation of the eternal processes of life and he seeks to establish his own role within this historical situation in terms of a particular archetype.

From the outset of the novel Constant is presented as a rather incongruous individual. With dentures and varicose veins, and convinced that death is approaching, he pedals slowly into the area on a "handsome racing bike" (13). Despite the fact that he is employed by a rather sordid black-marketeer, his principal concerns are in the area of metaphysics and religion: all the books that he reads speak only of "what is not visible" (25). Such incongruities indicate that, like the marshlands into which he cycles—neither sea nor firm ground, eternally existent yet constantly changir —Constant is living in two worlds that he attempts to reconcile. He has been interested from his early days in both "life" and "what is transcendent in life" (18). He has enjoyed and continues to enjoy the life he has led, but at the same time he looks forward to the experience of death. Both the past and the present are important for Constant, but they take on their significance from their participation in the eternal realities of the universe and ultimately form one eternal present. Hence, like Susini's Maison des Marais, Constant is "a stranger to the present and yet an accomplice of all that time brings in its train" (18), he is "elsewhere, but also in the marshland" (25).

Constant's disillusionment with politics and his conviction of social decadence have led him to relate to the world of nature rather than to the world of men. In particular he is, like Gilles, attracted to the apparent emptiness of the deserts that he has encountered during his travels, since he is able to identify with the richness of the asceticism that they suggest. "He forever had in the depths of his soul the soul of the desert" (23).

His tendency to allow his consciousness to merge with the surrounding world of nature expresses itself on at least two occasions in the early pages of the novel. Lying in a hollow overlooking the marshes, Constant merges in his mind the words of the book he is reading and a tuft of dry salt grass with its message of eternity: "In his mind the words and the tuft were bound together. He was this bond and the world was this bond" (25). The self which unites in its consciousness these two transitory elements is itself seen as part of the world that contains it. Shortly afterward Constant comes upon Dr. Bardy making love to Roxane, the wife of Liassov, a Russian painter living in the area. Unable to retreat without attracting attention, he finds himself obliged to stand and watch. As Constant's mind wanders, the incident loses its particularity: he has before him Adam and Eve in Eden, and from here his attention moves to the creation myths of other cultures. But these mythological generalizations of one of the basic acts of life do not remain exterior to Constant's self and he has the impression that the self is projected into a wider realm in which its individuality is obscured:

> It was no longer a question of a man and a woman, or even of two bodies; it was no longer even a question of the childish conjunction of worlds, of cosmic rendez-vous, flirtations or chattering. No, it was something in the depths of Constant's person—which was not part of these depths and which was not Constant. Constant fascinated by himself, the "moi" precipitated into the "soi," the world descending into that point from which it emerged and which has nothing to do with it, God eternally alien to God. God eternally abolishing his name. (36–37)

Ultimately the individuality of the creator, be it God Himself, fades into the anonymity of the eternal.

It is within this context that Constant is attracted to the art of the painter, in which he sees expressed the desired conjunction of the transitory and the eternal. The painter, better than any other, is able to "accept the ephemeral and to consecrate the ephemeral," to capture "the infinite in a stroke" and to "encrust the eternal into the daily round" (100). Such an ideal is suggested during the first encounter between Constant and Liassov. Wandering into the painter's hut among the dunes, Constant is startled to find a fresco grouping Buddha, Osiris, Dionysos, Christ, Athys, Orpheus, and Mahomet. Impressed by the manner in which the artist has combined human and nonhuman elements in his work, Constant expresses the thought that has for some time been establishing itself in his mind and exclaims: "Here, complete atheism engenders the purest sense of the divine" (51). Here too the divine, the eternal, or, as Constant later describes it, "the Inexpressible" (127), is conceived as involving the absorption not only of the individual's self but ultimately of the selfhood of God.

Although Constant believes his mind is now "beyond history" (109), the assignment given him by Susini necessitates the contact with Préault, Salis, Bardy, and Cormont. The pressures exerted by these individuals threaten the political neutrality that he had imagined employment by a black-marketeer would bring. Fidelity to Susini as employer has up till now been for him "the measure of his indifference to everyone and to Susini himself" (208), but such indifference is no longer possible.

Constant's means of reconciling the political involvement forced upon him with his attitude of political and moral indifference is to view the situation from a much wider perspective. The actors in this petty drama of wartime France are depicted as playing out, on a wider stage, a tragedy of profound religious significance to Western man, one which has "eternal" ramifications. In this way Constant is enabled to preserve the distance he desires while playing a significant role in the immediate situation.

Decadent twentieth-century France is assimilated in Constant's eyes to the Jewish nation in the first century A.D. With the glorious days of David and Solomon receding ever further into the past, the Jews, like their modern counterparts, are under the heel of an invader. Bardy, Salis, and Préault represent the various reactions to the foreign occupation, while Cormont is cast in the role of Jesus, one who, as Son of David, excites the hopes and heightens the expectations of those still willing to believe in the possibility of national greatness. Constant sees himself more and more clearly as Judas the betrayer. Obsessed in his earlier years by hopes of national regeneration, Judas joins the disciples, since their leader, with the apparently earthly kingdom that he speaks of, provides the best focus for his hopes. Under the influence of the disciple John, however, Judas is conceived by Constant as gradually acquiring a less active and more spiritual conception of the Messiah. Certain sections of the Old Testament indicate to him that suffering and death are necessary for the Messiah's function as Savior to be fulfilled, so that he prepares to offer himself as traitor and executioner. That Cormont is unaware of the "eternal" aspects of his nationalistic aspirations is not of major concern to Constant. The young man remains the incarnation of the glorious France which once existed and which will be enshrined in eternity through the sacrifice of his death. That is why, at the end of the novel, Constant plans to destroy Cormont together with the arms and ammunition that probably symbolize France's remaining resources during the wartime occupation. Constant's conception of the momentous act of betrayal and execution has, moreover, the added advantage that the sacrificial act also involves the annihilation or dispersal of the individual self.

Sacrifice consequently assumes, as in *L'Homme à cheval,* a position of central importance in the novel: Constant refers to it at one point as the center and the essence of human destiny (221). Even before he has begun to think deeply about Judas, Constant is aware that his thoughts have been leading him to "a central realization which truly would bring confirmation to his life, introduce to it that sacred definitive element without which it seemed to him that it would not have been lived and would not have found its fundamental eternal nature" (47–48). In this early definition of the dimly glimpsed "central realization" of his life, Constant moves from "life" to the "sacred," thence to "eternity." It is these three elements that the idea of sacrifice finally enables him to link. Sacrifice is a sacred act in that, paradoxically, in the very act of destruction the worth of the sacrifice is both affirmed and related to a world beyond the transitory one from which it is drawn. Hence, by sacrificing Cormont as an incarnation of a glorious idea of France, associating himself with this act, and indeed sacrificing himself at the same time, Constant, as Judas, is achieving all his goals.

Since Cormont's ideals, though labeled naive and anachronistic, are ultimately glorified, Frédéric Grover is justified in his remark that "Drieu's last novel expresses his ineradicable nationalism." By enabling the transitory and the eternal to achieve a point of juncture, Constant is according his traitorous act transcendent value: he is fulfilling his earlier expressed wish to unite thought and action at the moment of dying (26); and, like Judas, he is enabling the path of salvation to be opened. Finally by sacrificing himself, Constant is protesting against a decadent society, affirming the worth of the life which he has lived and at the same time destroying the superficialities of the self. A few moments before his death Constant reflects: "Is killing Constant Trubert the same as killing me? No, it's killing this individual, this bore that I have been dragging around after me for the past fifty years. It's killing my shadow, everything in me that is superfluous and cumbersome . . ." (238).

One of the most interesting formal aspects of the novel is the gradual and tentative manner in which Constant's "solution" is presented. In investigating the world of myth and religion and seeking to apply his discoveries to a contemporary situation, Drieu takes the reader into his confidence, shares with him his uncertainties and misgivings and creates a distance from his central character whenever close identification becomes a temptation. In particular there is considerable hesitation expressed about the apparent abandonment by Constant of the this-worldly approach to religion and life advocated by Nietzsche. Constant strives to reconcile the doctrines of Nietzsche, whom he respects, with an interest in a transcendent world. He does so to his own satisfaction, but only at the cost of presenting Nietzsche as a representative modern decadent. At one stage he addresses himself as a "derisory

Nietzschean, derisory like all Nietzscheans in the West, derisory like Nietzsche himself" (153). This attitude provokes the author's comment that "Constant ended up by misunderstanding the personal greatness of Nietzsche" (154) and arouses the earlier expressed suspicion that Constant is unable to "give reality in himself to the twofold Nietzschean concept of freedom" (128). However, the author's distance and detachment from Constant and his ideas appear at their most extreme and at their most spectacular in the final paragraph of the novel. In response to Constant's hysterical outpourings about blood and sacrifice as he prepares to perform the supreme act of his life, the author echoes the sentiments of the novel's epigraph and snuffs out Constant and his companions before the act can be performed: "Heaven and earth are not human or benevolent after the manner of men, they consider all beings as if they were straw dogs who have served in sacrifices" (7).

Although *Les Chiens de paille* stands clearly in the line of Drieu's continuing meditation on the place and function of the self in a decadent society, it is in many respects an experimental novel. The religious traditions of East and West are clearly assuming growing importance in Drieu's thinking, and this work represents his first—and unhappily the last—attempt to give them acceptable literary form in a contemporary situation. The author's extremely self-conscious detachment from Constant that we have noted above is one indication of his uncertainty about using these traditions for purposes of literary creation. It is probably this uncertainty which accounts for one of the major faults of this work of fiction: the unacceptably large amount of space accorded to philosophical and religious discourse. Despite their overall relevance to the subject of the novel and their intrinsic interest, Constant's excursions into religious history and philosophy are not nearly so well incorporated into the story as, for example, in the last section of *L'Homme à cheval.* Having achieved a high standard of excellence in the more traditional forms of the novel represented by *Gilles* and *L'Homme à cheval,* Drieu is obviously feeling his way in a new mode of expression. His next novel, which his death left unfinished, resembles *Les Chiens de paille* in that the hero's life is interpreted in terms of the life of another man. In conception, however, it is rather more modest than its predecessor and the philosophical speculation it contains is far less obtrusive.

Mémoires de Dirk Raspe

In his diary of July 29, 1944, Drieu expressed his desire to write a novel "which would tie in with *Les Chiens de paille.*" He went on to specify that the link between the works would be the theme of "initiates who fail" and that the background to the novel, the "ground plan," would be the life of Van Gogh. In the following October Drieu began the realization of this project and in the remaining months of that year he produced the four parts of *Mémoires de Dirk Raspe* [Memoirs of Dirk Raspe]. The work is incomplete since mental depression in the early months of 1945 and his suicide in mid-March prevented him from undertaking the remaining three parts. Publication of the manuscript did not occur until 1966.

The principal preoccupations of Dirk Raspe are, as for Constant Trubert, aesthetic and religious in nature. The "ephemeral" and the "eternal" are for him inextricably intertwined and interdependent, and the four periods of his life presented in the novel may each be seen as an attempt to manifest this basic truth, at first only half-consciously but then with growing conviction. The amorality and political indifference of a Constant are now replaced by a developing consciousness of the importance of art, particularly the visual art of painting, in uniting in the one creation the complementary aspects of the seen and the unseen. Consequently this novel does not merely take up certain of the philosophical issues of *Les Chiens de paille* and provide a keener, more literary focus for them. It also continues the reflections begun in *L'Homme à cheval* on the nature of artistic activity and of the artistic imagination.

The events of Dirk Raspe's life, especially in the first part, correspond only very loosely to what is known of Van Gogh. Initially we find him in his teenage years living in the English countryside with a clergyman and his family whom he observes closely. Richard Heywood is a rather dilatory pastor, fulfilling his meager functions in such a way as not to disturb his parishioners with new ideas or unorthodox actions. His intelligent, active wife, Louise, writes his sermons for him, while he, neglecting the books that line the shelves of his library, shows greater interest in entomology and botany, in the divine wonders of butterflies and flowers, than in the more strictly theological aspects of his vocation. But now even his interest in the natural world has faded and he appears to float somewhere between earth and sky, a state conveyed by the pale blue of his eyes: "Was this the blue of the water, or of the sky? More limpid than water, shimmering more than the sky" (19). Robert, the eldest son, is similar to his father in general appearance, but his blue eyes betray an individual of apparently quite a different order: "With Robert the blue was clouded, as it were; you could imagine that in him the blue had a basic quality. There was also a piercing spark in that blue, which was quite absent from the blue of the father" (19). On several occasions the blueness of his eyes is described as "cold." Also a clergyman, Robert has a parish in a poor working-class area of Birmingham and sees Christianity solely in terms of providing practical help to those in need. He considers theology and biblical exegesis to be dead and irrelevant and shuns them to promote his Socialist ideas that have already earned him the disapproval of his bishop. Cyril, the second son, has likewise taken on his father's profession but has quite different views from his brother. His interest in the things of the spirit is far deeper, and the blue of his eyes has a warmer quality that recalls the intensity of his mother. For Cyril charity is not necessarily the most pressing activity for the Christian to undertake and he relates rather to the mystics in the Church's history. Cyril introduces the theme of art into the novel and it is also he who stresses the importance of self-knowledge: "You can look at yourself in the mirror and still deceive yourself; people never look at themselves long enough" (25).

Dirk is a boarder in this family for ten years and is extremely sensitive to the varying influences it offers. He does not identify himself as a first person narrator until halfway through Part I, his introduction of himself as a character in the story coinciding with the presentation of the differences of opinion between Robert and Cyril. Dirk is attracted to the ideas of both sons and speaks of them later as "the pillars of my mythology" (107). Moreover, in a statement which prefigures both the torments of his later life and the development of his conception of art, he describes himself as being for the brothers "the place that their profound quarrel had chosen" (37). At this stage such conflict is welcomed and interiorized by Dirk, and it continues to simmer until it issues in a view of life and art that embraces both elements in somewhat uneasy synthesis. Such a resolution of the brothers' conflict is glimpsed in Dirk's exclamation to Cyril: "There is in Robert the same love of beauty as there is in you, and in you the same love of the human as there is in him" (44). The full ramifications of this discovery, however, come only later with the personal experience of artistic creation.

Within the context of this family of Anglican clergymen, the dispute between Cyril and Robert is cast in terms of Christian theology and fidelity to the Christian ethic. With his Calvinist background Dirk largely adopts such terminology but, encouraged by Cyril, he is perceptive enough to see beyond it to the more general and basic aspects of life to which it refers. Is God to be sought by a constant attempt to escape the self through preoccupation either with nature or with other men? Is Robert correct when he castigates self-expression in art as "playing with the suffering of others" (27)? Or on the other hand is awareness of God, which may eventually prove of greater value to man than charity, to be gained by an even deeper probing of the self in order to discover its nature and possibilities as well as its links with the outside world? Is Cyril, when speaking of his father, justified in saying to Robert: "You are fleeing from the Church and even from God through your poor just as he is through his flowers" (26)? Is he right in detecting in his father and brother an unwillingness to seek God within the reality of the self? As he asks himself these questions Dirk gradually becomes aware that the self is a reality that is ultimately inescapable (34).

Torn between the moral appeal of Robert and the more philosophical attitude of Cyril, Dirk takes his first steps as an artist. His drawings are technically weak, but they represent a significant stage in his development and portray the unresolved conflicts in his mind. The dominating subject is the poverty that Robert strives to alleviate in Birmingham, but Cyril is careful to point out that they also show something within the artist that is worthy of expression and needs to be cultivated. Thus by the end of the first part of the novel Dirk has become the battleground of the brothers' ideas in rather more tangible fashion: albeit imperfectly and largely unconsciously, he has transferred the conflict to the realm of pictorial art. He wonders at the significance and validity of this attempt at self-expression and spends his later years in rather extreme efforts to find an answer.

Part II finds Dirk some years later in the employ of a London art dealer, Phillip Mack. Here he comes into contact with a number of artists and grows more discriminating in his judgment of artistic merit. As his critical powers and technical competence develop, he becomes increasingly impatient with the artistic standards of those who paint for his employer and buy from him, and he also comes to doubt the merit of many others who have achieved celebrity. At first attracted by Meissonier, he comes to reject him because "his soul has nothing to tell, it has neither desires nor torments" (69). This harsh judgment indicates not only that Cyril's conception of art as the expression of the deepest recesses of the self has not been forgotten by Dirk, but also that for him this self has life and creativity only insofar as it expresses stress and dissatisfaction. Dirk's obsession with light and shade—and in particular his stress on the conflict between day and night in the Genesis Creation story (76)—may be viewed in these terms.

Conflict within the reality of the person is, however, precisely what people seek to hide or avoid, preferring those works in which the self is silent. Dirk has an extremely personal experience of this preference when he sketches a prostitute whose face and figure had attracted him on the London streets. Feeling that for the first time he is truly inspired, he loses sight of the reality of the woman before him and produces an intensely personal vision that has little apparent resemblance to his model. Convinced that she would be disappointed with the "portrait," he quickly sketches something that is more conventional but artistically worthless and she goes off satisfied.

Such experiences and his growing familiarity with the great masters bring Dirk to a belief that art is essentially a transfiguration of reality, a personal vision using the images of the imagination. He adopts this point of view in his drawing with the enthusiasm of a neophyte, and indeed to such a degree that he finds himself completely losing touch with the reality of people and things, and reducing them to the enclosed artistic world of image, line, and color. A brick wall becomes a mere patch of color, its concrete reality devoured by what he terms his "de luxe imagination":

> My appetite was terrible and devastating, yes, devastating, for I took no account of the things in themselves, but rather of what they must allow me to wrench from them so that I could compose images in which they would perhaps not find those features that were dearest to them and which for me were precisely not their fundamental characteristics. (79)

For one who aspires to a synthesis of the attitudes of the two Heywood brothers a reaction is inevitable. Without abandoning his attachment to the views of Cyril, Dirk becomes aware that the color and form which he has extracted from the people and things he paints have themselves become lifeless and artificial because deprived of the forces that inspired them: "By relishing colors and forms, I had imagined I was grasping the reality behind the appearance; now all that was reversed, it was the colors that threatened to be appearances. [. . .] So there were humans, I had forgotten human beings" (106). The views of Cyril on art have been adopted far too readily and his first essay into the world of art has left him once again confronted by "the obstacles of appearance" (103). In consequence Dirk determines to launch himself into the arena of human misery and folly so that a fuller understanding of the life of men may enrich his personal vision of reality.

Part III recounts the period which Dirk spends as an evangelist in the poor mining town of Hoeuvre in Belgium. This is a time characterized by what he later terms "obscurity of confusion" (137) and such uncertainty is evident in the description of both his thoughts and his actions. With his customary tendency to take extreme measures, Dirk begins by attempting to bury himself in the wretchedness of human misery so that he may crucify the aspects of the self that distress him: "Above all I wanted to refuse nothing of what was wounding and tormenting me, but on the contrary make it penetrate to my very bones" (115). Only slowly does he emerge from this confused psychological state to achieve a heightened awareness of his relationship to others and also of the nature of art, which he has at this point abandoned.

Dirk fails in his frantic attempts to lose and forget himself in well-doing and personal privation among the poor. Gradually he is forced to confront the "unyielding and obscure element" (116) which he senses Robert Heywood had discovered after similar work in the slums of Birmingham. Francis, one of the miners, and ugly like Dirk himself, startles him with the statement: "You have come among them, but you look beyond them, into yourself" (145). This brings Dirk to a recollection of his earlier attitudes to the inescapability of the self. For a time he is unwilling to face the implications of this illumination and in a frenzy born of desperation he devotes himself to the care of the sick during an epidemic, moving feverishly "among the typhus like a devil in his hell" (146). Finally, however, in conversation with another miner, Joos, he is forced to a recognition of the primacy of the self and says: "At bottom, I do not want to save the souls of others, but my own. At bottom, others are only a pretext, a means" (148–49). The goal of union of the self with the selves of others as a manifestation of the unity of all life is retained. However, as Camilla Bustamente also learned from the lips of Jaime, such union is possible only when the task of one's own self-realization has been accomplished.

Shortly afterwards Cyril Heywood is reintroduced into the narrative to encourage Dirk in this line of thinking and to recall him to his vocation as artist. Although Cyril describes himself as a "failed poet" (160), Dirk finds in him a sense of certainty that suggests self-realization and self-accomplishment. Through him and the poetry that he reads, Dirk comes to an awareness that God is to be found not at the end of the self's quest for union with others and the world but at the very center of the self. This discovery, moreover, paradoxically abolishes distinctions of self and nonself. God is, he says, "that liquor which discharges itself into my heart and which is made of the substance of my heart, which ravages and destroys my heart and which remains only as intoxication in the place where my heart was" (163–64). In this light, art takes on greater significance for Dirk, becoming an expression by the self of the oneness of "the heart of man and the heart of the world" (163), an expression of the normally unrecognized unity of existence. In the terms of such a vision, art becomes identified with ultimate reality—"art alone exists" (164) as Dirk expresses it in a moment of exaltation—and his earlier statement to the uncomprehending Joos that "a saint can only be an artist" (154) takes on fuller meaning.

In the closing pages of Part III vivid pictorial expression is given to the creative tumult of Dirk's mind and to his illumination on the nature of art by the description of a violent storm to which he exposes himself as he wanders the open plain surrounding Hoeuvre. Highly poetic and at times ecstatic in tone, this description first evokes Dirk's new found vision of unity. Sensing that the depth of his experience at Hoeuvre has enabled him to incorporate in himself both the world of man and the reality of the countryside, he offers himself as a sacrifice to the fury of the elements. It is his hope that the lightning from on high will penetrate him and so accomplish in him the full unity of creation to which he aspires. The desired act of sacrifice does not take place, but, in the periodic illumination of the countryside brought about by the lightning flashes, Dirk comes to share the vision of those painters who have glimpsed the unity that sacrifice was to have manifested: "The awesome creative light that sculpts the night, makes form spring forth, the light that snatches a vision from the night, the light of painters, the light of Rembrandt, of Delacroix! And the light of musicians, the light of artists" (169). Having traversed the worlds of Robert and Cyril and explored their extremities, Dirk is ready to return to the world of art with a fuller understanding of the nature of his vocation.

The period spent by Dirk in the Hague at the age of twenty-nine and thirty forms the subject of the novel's fourth and final part. It is a period marked by growing confidence in his ability as an artist, consolidation of the conception that he holds of the nature and significance of his work, and awareness of the difficulties of his vocation. His conviction of the unity of the world, which he has always carried with him as an instinct (55), now helps him to take less account of ugliness in himself and others, and this allows a deeper, more conscious penetration to the soul of those whom he sketches and paints. The prostitute "Tristesse," with whom he lives for some time and who serves as a model for him, recognizes this new intensity of vision by her remark: "you are interested in what people really are" (196). Dirk, moreover, notes the new attitude he has toward himself: "My interest in myself was only in what went right beyond the limits of a personality in the usual sense of the word, to what in me was reflective, dreamed, transcended all bounds, departed from the normal, blended with the obscure nameless forces or with what bore dangerously vague and deceptive names: God, the soul, love" (182). Through his painting he discovers in himself the various individuals he has been in his life, and he continues to extend the experience he has gained by nourishing himself at the "most general, generous sources of life" (183).

Dirk's need of close contact with men both to feed his creative talent and to fulfill his artist's function as a link between the self and the nonself paradoxically leads to alienation from others and a progressive distancing of himself from a civilization which prizes the superficial. He finds little in common with the painters and art dealers with whom he has contact and from whom he learns points of technique. The successful young Stavelot paints only elegant women and delicate interiors, and for Dirk his work lacks the depth and the conflict necessary to make it an adequate expression of the self; old Tulp, a distant cousin and a competent painter, initially excites Dirk's respect and affection, but, as Dirk's standards become more demanding, he dismisses him delicately but firmly with the remark: "Well armed to speak the truth he had no truth to speak, except that which any worthy fellow can make his own" (182).

Perhaps the most distressing example of the alienation that closer acquaintance brings is to be found in Dirk's relationship with two women: Tristesse, who comes from the very dregs of society, and his beautiful middle-class cousin Catherine. Largely transpositions of Conchita and Camilla in *L'Homme à cheval,* these two women represent the beautiful and the ugly in Dirk's experience of life. Moreover, his successive associations with them indicate his need to reconcile the apparent antinomy between them and to find beauty in each circumstance. In this context it is significant that on numerous occasions Dirk should state his admiration of Baudelaire and his "Flowers of Evil" and that (like Constant Trubert) he should establish himself in a depressing area of "marshland and sand" from which he strives to extract "all the beauty of the world" (220). "Nothing is ugly" (210), cries Dirk to Tristesse, who is painfully conscious of her shortcomings, while to Catherine, who finds his painting sad and depressing, he exclaims: "But there is beauty in everything and where there is beauty, there is joy" (225). There is, however, no answering chord to these sentiments in either woman. Catherine refuses his offer of marriage and remains in her superficial bourgeois world, while Tristesse leaves him to enter a *maison close* ("brothel"). Ultimately both belong to the same superficial world from which Dirk is progressively alienating himself. His experiences lead him to conclude that "[our whole civilization] appears to be grasping everything with a bold and wasteful hand, but it is rejecting everything. It is rejecting almost the whole of life, spiritual richness" (215).

Tragically, the text of *Mémoires de Dirk Raspe* ends at this point. On March 15, 1944, Drieu lived out in his own life the predictable ending of Dirk's (Van Gogh's) earthly existence. In his preface to the novel, Pierre Andreu speculates, probably correctly, that the remaining three parts would have transposed into Dirk's life Van Gogh's experience in Paris, Arles, and Auvers prior to his suicide. Frédéric Grover's belief that Drieu would have intruded into the narrative as author in a similar way to Geneviève Le Pesnel in *Rêveuse bourgeoisie* seems a little less likely. However this may be, the four parts that we possess, despite their speed of composition and relative lack of authorial revision, are among Drieu's finest achievements as a writer. In contrast to *Les Chiens de paille,* the richness of his philosophical thought finds a highly appropriate vehicle for expression in the life and work of the painter whom Liassov had described in the earlier work as "wise to the point of madness" (54). The tormented life of the Dirk Raspe–Van Gogh figure enables Drieu to explore the mysteries of his own reality and his relationship to the world, while the inspiration of Van Gogh's painting contributes to the highly effective stress on color in the novel and to the rich and daring imagery of such scenes as the storm at Hoeuvre. That Drieu found such adaptation of a model a liberating experience is indicated by an entry in his diary on October 28, 1944, when he writes: "I am tracing a new image of my freedom." By identifying, through his fictional characters, with perceptive but alienated individuals from the past (the "initiates who fail," mentioned in his diary), first Judas, then Van Gogh, Drieu apparently found considerable release from the constrictions of his age and his political circumstances and also a fresh exhilarating understanding of his role as an artist in language. The existence of an as yet unpublished manuscript of a play entitled *Judas* suggests that Drieu would have pursued this path in his later writing.

Chapter Seven
Conclusion

Drieu's imaginative writings of the interwar period show different attempts to investigate and to relate two constant thematic elements: the self, with its Romantic aspirations to the absolute; and the imperfect decadent society in which this self is set. The investigation of these two elements takes many forms. Attempts to gain historical perspective in *Rêveuse bourgeoisie* and *Gilles* accompany the synchronic approach of such works as *Plainte contre inconnu* and *Blèche*; first person narration in *Etat civil* and *La Comédie de Charleroi* alternates with the relatively objective third-person narration of *Journal d'un homme trompé* and *Une femme à sa fenêtre;* the lyrical outpouring of *Interrogation* contrasts with the gloomy, disabused reflections of the hero of *Le Feu follet*; and the exotic elements of *Beloukia* are set amid the dullness of contemporary French society that is castigated in most of the other works. The resulting body of literature, to which Frédéric Grover attaches the name "literature of testimony," gives a many-faceted but highly individualistic vision of the age. It is, however, a vision with which some of the most perceptive and sensitive minds of the period have been able to identify. François Mauriac, for example, spoke in these terms of Drieu in 1958: "Drieu was at the center, not at the political center, but at the nervous center, at the magnetic center of the attractions and temptations of a generation. He felt very keenly all the currents, all the forces that passed through an entire age."[1]

The main attraction of Drieu's works for the present-day reader, however, does not lie so much in their presentation of a particular interpretation of a fascinating historical period. It is to be found rather in the writer's imaginative efforts to face the enduring problem of how an individual relates to a society considered distasteful and decadent. Within the context of Drieu's vision of the interwar period the attempt to relate brings only dissatisfaction, frustration, and moral degradation.

The male self which traces its unhappy path through Drieu's fiction is deeply influenced by the decadence of the age and proves inadequate in matters of love as it demands from its partners greater vitality and commitment than it can itself provide. The catalog of sexual misery contained in *Journal d'un homme trompé* amply illustrates the situation as the author sees it. Contemporary political life, perhaps most vividly portrayed through Chanteau and his Radicals in *Gilles,* successfully resists attempts at change and alienates the efforts of those individuals with enterprise and courage enough to demand something better. The moral effects on those unable to adapt to the lack of challenge in political and social life are depicted most clearly in *Le Feu follet,* but also appear through Camille in *Rêveuse bourgeoisie.* The option sought by Blaquans in *Blèche:* intellectual and moral isolation, is, on the other hand, completely rejected as "bad faith," as a refusal to face the problems of life in society.

Only in the illumination of the charge at Charleroi does the eagerly sought unity between the self and the world prove possible. Here the self is experienced as fulfilled since momentarily it incorporates the richness of the world. The experience takes place outside normal society, however, and is, within the context of modern warfare, as rare and fleeting as a woman's separation from the values of her society.

The complexity of Drieu's presentation of the relationship between the self and society is seen most clearly through the character of Gille(s), who appears in three novels and numerous short stories. Afflicted by the inner demands of an idealistic self which seeks in life an experience of the absolute—a rather more dynamic version of Proust's "privileged moment"—Gille(s) finds himself conditioned in childhood and influenced in his adult life by social values which he instinctively rejects. This accounts for the sense of "lostness" which so mystifies yet attracts those with whom Gille(s) associates and which continues to exercise its fascination more than fifty years after the character's conception. A form of Barresian "déraciné," Gille(s) reflects some of the enigmatic qualities of Watteau's painting, which, as Dominique Desanti points out,[2] bears a striking resemblance to Drieu himself!

The importance assumed by art and sacrifice in the three novels of the war years represents the ultimate and most significant stage in Drieu's efforts to reconcile the claims of the self and the facts of man's social and metaphysical situation. In common with his close friend André Malraux, Drieu, in the early 1940s, came to focus particular attention on the significance of artistic activity, especially in the visual arts. As early as 1934, in the first part of "Journal d'un délicat," we read: "For me, a picture is the articulation of a prayer, a magical means of attaining the beyond, in the midst of the here and now."[3] It is not until ten years later, however, in the pages of *Les Chiens de paille* and *Mémoires de Dirk Raspe* that the implications of this statement begin to be drawn out. Through the painting of Liassov and the different experiences that Dirk has in his formation as a painter, awareness comes that art, while firmly set in the world of man's activity, may serve as a means of access to the ideal world to which the self aspires. The same revelation, transposed to a different realm of art, may be inferred from *L'Homme à cheval*. Here its expression comes through the guitar and the experience of Felipe.

The theme of sacrifice, which dominates the closing pages not only of *Gilles* but also of *L'Homme à cheval* and *Les Chiens de paille,* and which would almost certainly have figured largely in the final sections of *Mémoires de Dirk Raspe* and the play *Judas,* emerges as a further means of achieving, at least symbolically, the elusive unity between the self and its social and metaphysical destiny. Gilles "finds himself" in an act of virtual suicide, which, by enabling thought and action to be finally linked, takes on the overtones of sacrifice. Similarly, Jaime's sacrifice of his horse Brave is conceived as a means of both affirming the ideal of action he has pursued in his social and political life and incorporating this social and political ideal into an eternal immutable world. Such a concept of sacrifice is pursued somewhat further in *Les Chiens de paille,* where the figure of Judas allows even closer incorporation of the individual: the role of traitor is willingly assumed as the path of human salvation; conscious human sacrifice of victim and priest replaces animal sacrifice; and the personal, the political, and the sacred are linked in an ultimate expression of the unity of creation.

Constant's mystical vision highlights the concept of unity underlying all Drieu's thinking. The itinerary of Drieu's fictional heroes reveals a mind which needed to "vibrate in unison with the world"[4] and which projected itself into literary creation to investigate the means by which this might be achieved. In consequence we have an everwidening conception of the self as it passes from relationships with family and school to those involving war, women, and politics before seeking to manifest in itself the fundamental processes of life. Within this general pattern the tensions between self and society that are encountered result from frustration at the disparity between an ideal unity and the claims of the relative: the desire for the unity of "dream" and "action" in the first line of *Interrogation* is reflected in the very conception of Jaime in *L'Homme à cheval*. It is, however, precisely this tension, with the ideal of unity that it presupposes, that constitutes the essence of Drieu's works and serves to illuminate the fascinating personality of one whom not long ago many thought history had discarded.

Notes and References

Preface

1. Frédéric J. Grover, Letter in *Le Magazine littéraire* (Paris), January 1979, p. 4.
2. Jacqueline Lévi-Valensi, *Les Critiques de notre temps et Camus* (Paris: 1970), p. 12.
3. Marcel Proust, *Contre Sainte-Beuve* (Paris: Pléiade, 1971), pp. 221–22.
4. For a discussion of the idea of decadence in Drieu's work see Robert Barry Leal, "L'Idée de décadence chez Drieu la Rochelle," *La Revue des langues vivantes* (Liège) 40, no. 4, (1974):325–40.
5. Marcel Arland, "*Etat civil* par Pierre Drieu la Rochelle," *Nouvelle revue française* (Paris), April 1922, p. 491.

Chapter One

1. Pierre Drieu la Rochelle, *Sur les écrivains* (Paris, 1964), p. 173.
2. Ibid., p. 40.
3. Ibid., p. 174.
4. At certain times later in his life Drieu was inclined to play down the importance of violence in *Interrogation*. In a letter to Benjamin Crémieux published in the *Nouvelle revue française* in 1929, for example, he dismisses his youthful glorification of this aspect of war as "bookish imagination" and "intellectual lyricism" and concludes by classifying *Interrogation* as "a somewhat suspect writing that I shall have to rectify with another."
5. Drieu la Rochelle, *Sur les écrivains*, p. 177.
6. In *Récit secret* (Paris, 1961), composed in the last months of his life, Drieu acknowledges the "masochism of my youth" and refers to it as "that lascivious inversion" (p. 44).
7. Bernard Vorge, "Drieu la Rochelle ou le sacrifice," *Défense de l'Occident* (Paris), No. 50 (February–March 1958), p. 60.
8. For an indication of Drieu's relationship with the Surrealists see his three letters to the Surrealists reproduced in *Sur les écrivains* and also the article by Bruno Pompili.
9. When the work was republished in 1941 in *Ecrits de jeunesse*, a number of major changes were made: the embarrassingly frank "Preamble"

was relegated to the end; the short stories "L'Aumône" and "Le seul bonheur" were omitted; several of the titles were changed, as was the order of presentation; and the division into seven sections was abandoned. Less sweeping changes were also made to *Interrogation* and *Fond de cantine.*

10. The editions to which pagination refers are indicated in the bibliography.

11. These words do not appear in *Ecrits de jeunesse* but are taken from the 1927 edition.

Chapter Two

1. Pierre Drieu la Rochelle, *Ecrits de jeunesse* (Paris, 1941), preface, p. 7.

2. *Adieu à Gonzague* was composed following the suicide of Drieu's friend Jacques Rigaut, on whom Gonzague of "La Valise vide" was patterned.

3. Drieu la Rochelle, *Ecrits de jeunesse,* p. 204.

4. Frédéric J. Grover, *Drieu la Rochelle and the Fiction of Testimony* (Berkeley and Los Angeles, 1958), p. 95.

5. Pierre-Henri Simon, *Histoire de la littérature française au XXe siècle* (Paris: Colin, 1956), pp. 118–19.

Chapter Three

1. Colette, *Le Journal* (Paris), November 25, 1934.

2. Ramon Fernandez, "*Blèche,* par Drieu la Rochelle," *Nouvelle revue française* (Paris), December 1928, pp. 867–68.

3. For example: Ramon Fernandez, "*Une femme à sa fenêtre,* par Drieu la Rochelle," *Nouvelle revue française* (Paris) May 1930, pp. 767–69.

4. Grover, *Drieu la Rochelle and the Fiction of Testimony,* p. 89.

5. Pierre Drieu la Rochelle, "Signification sociale," *Revue du siècle* (Paris), July–August 1933, p. 91.

6. Allen Thiher, "Le Feu follet: the drug addict as a tragic hero," *PMLA,* January 1973, p. 38.

7. Frédéric J. Grover, "*Le Feu follet:* un roman qui fait encore peur," *Le Magazine littéraire* (Paris), December 1978, p. 28.

Chapter Four

1. Grover, *Drieu la Rochelle and the Fiction of Testimony,* pp. 113, 120.

2. Pierre Drieu la Rochelle, "A propos d'*A l'ouest rien de nouveau,*" *Nouvelle revue française* (Paris), November 1929, p. 730.

3. Quoted by Frédéric J. Grover, "Céline et Drieu la Rochelle," *Les Cahiers de l'Herne* (Paris), no. 3, (January 1963), p. 303.

4. Grover, *Drieu la Rochelle and the Fiction of Testimony,* p. 155.
5. Jean Vandal, "*Beloukia,* par Drieu la Rochelle," *Nouvelle revue française* (Paris), September 1936, p. 544.

Chapter Five

1. Quoted by Willy de Spens, "Drieu romancier," *La Parisienne* (Paris), no. 32 (October 1955), p. 1042.
2. Pol Vandromme, *Pierre Drieu la Rochelle* (Paris, 1958), p. 83.
3. Grover, *Drieu la Rochelle and the Fiction of Testimony,* p. 164.
4. In early February 1934, there were riots in Paris provoked by the apparent political protection afforded to a criminal, Serge Alexandre Stavisky. This incident encouraged the formation of the left-wing coalition known as the Popular Front, which came to power under Léon Blum in 1936.
5. Pierre Drieu la Rochelle, *Genève ou Moscou* (Paris, 1928), p. 15.

Chapter Six

1. Pierre-Henri Simon, "Drieu la Rochelle ou la tragédie manquée," *Revue générale belge* (Brussels), no. 60 (October 1950), p. 883.
2. Grover, *Drieu la Rochelle and the Fiction of Testimony,* p. 213.
3. Pierre Drieu la Rochelle, *Les Chiens de paille* (Paris, 1964), preface, p. 10.

Chapter Seven

1. François Mauriac, "Présence de Drieu la Rochelle," *Défense de l'Occident* (Paris), no. 50 (February 1958), p. 20.
2. Dominique Desanti, *Drieu la Rochelle ou le séducteur mystifié* (Paris, 1978), back cover.
3. Pierre Drieu la Rochelle, *Histoires déplaisantes* (Paris, 1963), p. 31.
4. Julien Hervier, *Deux individus contre l'histoire: Drieu la Rochelle, Ernst Jünger* (Paris, 1978), p. 141.

Selected Bibliography

Unless otherwise indicated place of publication is Paris. Where more than one edition exists, the edition used is preceded by *.

PRIMARY SOURCES

1. Works by Drieu la Rochelle

*Interrogation.** Gallimard, 1917.

*Fond de cantine.** Gallimard, 1920.

Etat civil. Gallimard, 1921;*1977 (collection "L'Imaginaire").

Mesure de la France. Grasset, 1922;*1964 (+ *Ecrits 1939–1940*).

Plainte contre inconnu. Gallimard, 1924.

L'Homme couvert de femmes. Gallimard, 1925;*1977.

*La Suite dans les idées.** Au sans pareil, 1927.

Le jeune Européen. Gallimard, 1927; 1978 (+ *Genève ou Moscou*).

Blèche. *Gallimard, 1928; Lausanne: Editions Rencontre, 1964.

Genève ou Moscou. Gallimard, 1928; 1978 (+ *Le jeune Européen*).

La voix. Edouard Champion, 1929 (reprinted in *Journal d'un homme trompé*).

Une femme à sa fenêtre. Gallimard, 1929;*1976.

L'Europe contre les patries. Gallimard, 1931.

Le Feu follet. Gallimard, 1931; 1963 (+ *Adieu à Gonzague*);* "Livre de poche" no. 2199; "Folio" no. 152.

L'Eau fraîche. Les Cahiers de Bravo, supplement August 1931.

Drôle de voyage. Gallimard, 1933;*1977.

Journal d'un homme trompé. Gallimard, 1934; *1978 (+ "Le Mannequin").

La Comédie de Charleroi. Gallimard, 1934; *"Livre de poche" no. 2737.

Socialisme fasciste. Gallimard, 1934.

Beloukia. Gallimard, 1936.

Doriot ou la vie d'un ouvrier français. Saint Denis: Les Editions populaires françaises, 1936.

Rêveuse bourgeoisie. Gallimard, 1937; 1960; *"Folio" no. 620.

Avec Doriot. Gallimard, 1937.

Gilles. Gallimard, 1939 (censored); 1942; *"Livre de poche" no. 831–832; "Folio" no. 459.

*Ecrits de jeunesse (Interrogation, Fond de cantine, La Suite dans les idées, *Le jeune Européen,* "Défense de sortir"). Gallimard, 1941.
Ne plus attendre. Grasset, 1941 (reprinted in *Chronique politique 1934–1942*).
Notes pour comprendre le siècle. Gallimard, 1941.
Chronique politique 1934–1942. Gallimard, 1943.
L'Homme à cheval. Gallimard, 1943; Club des librairies de France, 1962; *"Livre de poche" no. 1473; "Folio" no. 484.
Charlotte Corday; Le Chef. Gallimard, 1944.
Le Français d'Europe. Editions Balzac, 1944 (seized and destroyed).
Les Chiens de paille. Gallimard, 1944 (seized and destroyed); *1964.
Plaintes contre inconnue. Frédéric Chambriand, 1951 (withdrawn from sale).
Récit secret. A.M.G., 1951 (noncommercial distribution of 500 copies); *Gallimard, 1961 (+ *Journal* [1944–1945] and *Exorde*).
Histoires déplaisantes. Gallimard, 1963.
Sur les écrivains. Gallimard, 1964.
Mémoires de Dirk Raspe. *Gallimard, 1966; "Folio" no. 1042.
Les derniers jours (reprint). Editions Jean-Michel Place, 1979.
Nous sommes plusieurs (unpublished play).

2. English Translation of Works by Drieu la Rochelle
(La Comédie de Charleroi) The Comedy of Charleroi and Other Stories. Translated by Douglas Gallagher. Cambridge, Eng.: Rivers Press, 1973.
(Une femme à sa fenêtre) Hotel Acropolis. Translated by Patrick Kirwan. London: Nash and Grayson, 1931.
(Le Feu follet) The Fire Within. Translated by Richard Howard. New York: Knopf, 1965; Toronto: Random House, 1965.
(Le Feu follet) Will o' the Wisp. Translated by Martin Robinson. London: Calder and Boyars, 1966.
(L'Homme à cheval) The Man on Horseback. Translated by Thomas M. Hines. Columbia, S.C.: French Literature Publications, 1979.
(Récit secret) Secret Journal and Other Writings. Translated by Alistair Hamilton. Cambridge, Eng.: Rivers Press, 1973; New York: H. Fertig, 1974.

SECONDARY SOURCES

1. Selected Critical Works on Drieu la Rochelle

Andreu, Pierre. *Drieu, témoin et visionnaire.* Grasset, 1952. First full-length study of Drieu; strong biographical emphasis.

———, and Grover, Frédéric J. *Drieu la Rochelle.* Hachette, 1979. Most authoritative biography to date.

Cadwallader, Barrie. *Crisis of the European Mind. A Study of André Malraux and Drieu la Rochelle.* Cardiff: University of Wales Press, 1981. Useful background material. Surveys the intellectual climate of the interwar period in France.

Desanti, Dominique. *Drieu la Rochelle ou le séducteur mystifié.* Flammarion, 1978. Good for social and political background.

Frank, Bernard. *La Panoplie littéraire.* Julliard, 1958. Attempts to destroy the "mythology" surrounding Drieu.

Grover, Frédéric J. *Drieu la Rochelle.* Gallimard, 1962; revised 1979 (Collection "Idées"). Excellent introduction to Drieu.

———. *Drieu la Rochelle and the Fiction of Testimony.* Berkeley, Los Angeles: University of California Press, 1958. Still the best general work on Drieu as a literary artist.

———. *Six entretiens avec André Malraux sur des écrivains de son temps. (1959–1975).* Gallimard, 1978. Casts interesting light on Malraux's view of Drieu.

Hervier, Julien. *Deux individus contre l'histoire: Pierre Drieu la Rochelle, Ernst Jünger.* Klincksieck, 1978. Excellent comparative study; thematic in approach.

Hines, Thomas Moore. *"L'Homme à cheval" de Drieu la Rochelle. L'Anatomie d'un roman de transition.* Columbia, South Carolina: French Literature Publications, 1978. Focuses on genesis and principal themes of this novel, and on its relationship to Drieu's other works.

Kunnas, Tarmo. *Drieu la Rochelle, Céline, Brassillach et la tentation fasciste.* Les Sept couleurs, 1972. Comparative thematic study; many inaccuracies

Leal, Robert Barry. *Drieu la Rochelle: Decadence in Love.* St. Lucia, Australia: University of Queensland Press, 1973. Treats a key theme in Drieu's fiction.

Mabire, Jean. *Drieu parmi nous.* La Table ronde, 1963. A rather naively enthusiastic examination of Drieu's political (and religious) philosophy.

MacLeod, Alexander. *La Pensée politique de Pierre la Rochelle.* Editions Cujas, 1966. Short but useful study of Drieu's politics and the importance of myth.

Pérusat, Jean-Marie. *Drieu la Rochelle ou le goût du malentendu.* Frankfurt am/Main: Peter Lang, 1977. Sees Drieu's literature as deliberately obscuring (but nevertheless clearly reflecting) the author's ideological commitment to fascism.

Pompili, Bruno. *Pierre Drieu la Rochelle: Progetto e delusione.* Ravenna: Edizioni A. Longo, 1969. Discursive essay on various themes in Drieu; biographical approach.

Soucy, Robert. *Fascist intellectual: Drieu la Rochelle.* Berkeley, Los Angeles, London: University of California Press, 1979. Presents Drieu as a "fascist personality"; the approach is that of an historian and political scientist.

Vandromme, Pol. *Pierre Drieu la Rochelle.* Editions universitaires, 1958. Good introductory study; treats Drieu's attitudes to war, women, decadence, and politics.

2. Special Numbers of Periodicals Devoted to Pierre Drieu la Rochelle

La Parisienne. October 1955. Articles by Pierre Andreu, Jean Bernier, Jacques Chardonne, Lucien Combelle, Maurice Martin du Gard, Paul Morand, Michel Mourre, François Nourrissier, Willy de Spens.

Défense de l'Occident. February-March 1958. Articles by J.-M. Aimot, Pierre Andreu, Emmanuel Berl, Jean Bernier, J.-P. Bonnafous, P. Fieschi, Kléber Haedens, M. Jouhandeau, François Mauriac, Robert Poulet, Paul Sérant, Willy de Spens, Bernard Vorge.

Le Magazine littéraire. December 1978. Articles by Frédéric Grover, Julien Hervier, Pierre Andreu, Dominique Desanti, H. F. Rey, Jean-Marie Rouart.

3. Selected Critical Articles on Drieu la Rochelle

Arland, Marcel. "L'Épreuve." *Nouvelle revue française,* no. 14 (February 1954), pp. 279–88. (Also in his *La Grâce d'écrire.* Gallimard, 1955, pp. 166–76.)

Audiberti, Jacques. "A propos de *L'Homme à cheval.*" *Nouvelle revue française,* no. 352 (June 1943), pp. 744–57.

Boissard, J. M. de. "Drieu la Rochelle et la guerre." *Défense de l'Occident,* no. 83 (July-August 1969), pp. 51–65; no. 84 (September-October 1969), pp. 42–51.

Brasillach, Robert. "Drieu la Rochelle, toujours amer." In his *Les quatre jeudis.* Les sept couleurs, 1951, pp. 275–82.

Crémieux, Benjamin. "*La Suite dans les idées; Le jeune Européen; Les dernier jours,* par P. Drieu la Rochelle." *Nouvelle revue française,* no. 170 (November 1927), pp. 671–76.

Flagothier, François. "Le Point de vue dans l'oeuvre romanesque de Pierre Drieu la Rochelle." *Revue des langues vivantes,* 34th year, no. 2 (1968), pp. 170–83.

Girardet, Raoul. "Notes sur l'esprit d'un fascisme français 1934–1939." *Revue française de science politique,* no. 5 (June-September 1955), pp. 529–46.

Grover, Frédéric J. "Céline et Drieu la Rochelle." *Cahiers de l'Herne,* no. 3 (January 1963), pp. 302–305.

——— "Le dernier roman de Drieu la Rochelle," *Critique* 22 (May 1966): pp. 426–37.

——— "Malraux et Drieu la Rochelle." *Cahiers André Malraux I,* 1972, pp. 61–93. (*La Revue des lettres modernes,* nos. 304–309).

Hanrez, Marc. "Le dernier Drieu." *French Review* 43 (1970): 144–57. (Special Issue No. 1).

Joannon, Pierre. "Le Fascisme à travers Brasillach et Drieu la Rochelle." *Défense de l'Occident,'* no. 62 (April-May 1967): pp. 54–57.

Leal, Robert B. "Drieu la Rochelle and Malraux." *Australian Journal of French Studies* 10 (May–August 1973): 175–90.

——— "L'Idée de décadence chez Drieu la Rochelle." *Revue des langues vivantes* 40 (1974): 325–40.

Mabire, Jean. "Réflexions sur un Coutançais méconnu: Pierre Drieu la Rochelle." *Revue de la Manche,* July 1961, pp. 210–46; August 1961, pp. 293–332.

Martin du Gard, Maurice. "Les trois suicides de Drieu." *Revue des deux mondes,* no. 8 (August 1969), pp. 239–51.

Mauriac, François. "Drieu." *Table ronde,* no. 18 (June 1949), pp. 912–17.

M. E. (Mounier, Emmanuel). "Drieu la Rochelle: *Gilles.*" *Esprit,* 8th year, no. 91 (April 1940), pp. 87–90.

Pompili, Bruno. "Pierre Drieu la Rochelle e i surrealisti." *Studi Urbinati,* no. 1 (1968), pp. 164–90.

Soucy, Robert. "Le Fascisme de Drieu la Rochelle." *Revue d'histoire de la deuxième guerre mondiale,* no. 17 (April 1967), pp. 61–84.

Thiher, Allen. "*Le Feu follet:* The Drug Addict as a Tragic Hero." *PMLA* 88 (1973): 34–40.

Touvenel, Bruno. "Drieu la Rochelle: un itinéraire fasciste." *Défense de l'Occident,* March-April 1975, pp. 24–40.

Tucker, William R. "Fascism and Individualism: The Political Thought of Pierre Drieu la Rochelle," *Journal of Politics* 27 (1965): 153–77.

Van Den Bremt, Etienne. "L'Unité intérieure de Drieu la Rochelle." *Revue des langues vivantes* 33 (1967): 252–66.

Index